Seeing-Remembering-Connecting

Seeing-Remembering-Connecting

Subversive Practices of Being Church

☼

KAREN L. BLOOMQUIST

CASCADE *Books* · Eugene, Oregon

SEEING-REMEMBERING-CONNECTING
Subversive Practices of Being Church

Cascade Books
An Imprint of Wipf and Stock Publishers
199 W. 8th Ave., Suite 3
Eugene, OR 97401

www.wipfandstock.com

ISBN 13: 978-1-4982-8197-3

Cataloging-in-Publication data:

Bloomquist, Karen L.

Seeing-remembering-connecting : subversive practices of being church / Karen L. Bloomquist.

xiv + 108 p.; 23 cm—Includes bibliographical references.

ISBN 13: 978-1-4982-8197-3

1. Theology. 2. Church. 3. Christianity and politics. I. Title.

BX1746 B345 2016

Manufactured in the USA

Contents

An Autobiographical Preface

This book is rooted in and reflects what I have experienced and learned over the past half century. I continually have found myself in the swirling sometimes chaotic whirlwind of pivotal societal and ecclesial changes occurring during this time. I grew up in a church that was a stable, anchoring institution in both community and family. It embodied the importance of being a good citizen, upholding traditional values and a sense of social order, but with little conscious connection to emerging social challenges. In contrast to this in the late 1960s, I began to be exposed to the civil rights and peace movements, and the emerging woman's movement. Thus began a lifelong sojourn of what I have now come to frame as "seeing-remembering-connecting."

I intentionally sought out and began to see and experience what I had not before: blatant realities of exclusion, injustice and oppression. This was stirred up in high school through a critical social science teacher, as well as through daring leaders of the national (ALC) Luther League who drew us into stark realities and radical ways of thinking we would not have encountered otherwise. This was the beginning of "seeing" in new ways, apart from the conventional ways that still prevailed in a conservative Midwestern community. This continued during college, when as a result of an "urban plunge" summer experience in Chicago, I naively tried to open the eyes of those in my white home town to the realities of racism and the emerging Black Power movement.

Feeling drawn to participate in the first Global Semester of St. Olaf College, my eyes were opened as together we encountered the strange cultures and glaring injustices permeating the countries where we studied (Ethiopia, India, Thailand, and Japan). It was 1968–69, while the Vietnam War was raging, but we were being exposed to a much different side of these cultures and much different ideologies than those prevailing in the U.S. military. We were zealous to communicate what we had seen when we returned to communities that were still rather homogenous, but have become much more diverse since then.

Even at this stage, I was being drawn into a kind of remembering that was the inception of what would become a "re-membering." Lifted up and remembered were the prophetic traditions and social change trajectories in the Bible that often were overlooked, and which provide much of the impetus for social critique. Only much later, in graduate theological work, would I take up the challenge of "re-membering," that is, putting together or transfiguring theological traditions/themes in new ways. I began remembering what or who has been forgotten or overlooked in our own families, communities and churches, not to mention the rest of the world. I could not forget what I had seen throughout the world.

At the same time, increasingly I was caught up in the stirrings of the woman's movement, especially as it related to the church, which then was still a bastion of white male power and privilege. Although I had not previously thought of going to seminary, and received little encouragement from my all-male religion professors to do so, increasingly I felt drawn (now I realize "called") to do so, especially to a setting (Berkeley) where there was the possibility of connecting with a number of women ecumenically (but in 1970 not at Lutheran seminaries). I soon became coordinator of the fledgling women's center that was forming at the Graduate Theological Union. Although our critiquing of male-oriented language and theological constructs, advocating for the first women faculty to be hired, and early attempts to "do" feminist theology, may have appeared somewhat strident and/or naive to some, this *did* break through ground. Amazingly, in many places now over a majority or those studying at and teaching at theological seminaries are female, in dramatic contrast to 1970 when there was one or none.

During this time, I also became more aware of gay/lesbian stories and struggles, which still were being kept mostly silent, except in "safe" places like San Francisco, where since the 1960s church leaders had taken a lead in exposing this as a justice matter. While I was in seminary, the first openly gay pastor was ordained (1972 in the United Church of Christ). However, this did not become a more public struggle in the Evangelical Lutheran Church in America (ELCA) until 1988, when three gay men at the seminary from which I earlier had graduated became open. From then, it took until 2009 before ELCA policies changed.

I became increasingly focused on how church and society relate to each other, and critical of how that had been occurring in the aftermath of the 1950s. In retrospect it was not by coincidence that I majored in both religion and sociology in college, then chose to attend a seminary in Berkeley, and later pursued a doctorate at Union Theological Seminary in NYC, both in places at the cauldron of significant social changes that would soon be sweeping across and transforming the whole country and globe, and with teachers at the latter who were at the critical forefront of this, such as Dorothee Soelle, James Cone, Cornel West, Tom Driver, and Beverly Harrison.

"Connecting" can describe what I did in my doctoral dissertation, where I made critical links between the liberation and political theologies I had been drawn to, with the working class realities in my upbringing and first congregation. I had sometimes looked down upon the latter in my drive to become upwardly mobile, but this changed when I connected these realities with transformative insights from Lutheran theology viewed through liberation/political theologies.[1] Through this seeing and remembering, I began to make connections I had not before. I connected the faith traditions that had formed me with the pursuit of social justice and liberation, and connected with other groups pursuing this. I also began making connections—identifying the gaps or contradictions—between what was proclaimed and the actual

---

1. Bloomquist, *The Dream Betrayed.*

realities of injustice, between the official American creed and the realities of what actually was occurring in the wider society.

Significantly, what I saw and experienced in serving as the pastor of local congregations (in California, New York City, and Washington State) has been the point of reference and account-ability for much of my theological work. Furthermore, the theo-logical/pastoral method I developed was one where what ordinary folks actually were experiencing was connected critically with the official reigning scripts they had been conditioned to buy into, thus evoking what needed to be addressed theologically.

In the 1980s I moved with my husband Bill to Chicago where our son Aaron was born, and where I served on the faculty at the Lutheran School of Theology. Just as I was about to be tenured, I left that position because I felt called to direct the department through which various critical social issues would be addressed in the early years of Evangelical Lutheran Church in America (ELCA), and the opportunity to shape new more participatory ways for doing so. From the beginning of the ELCA in 1988, we envisioned the church becoming a community of moral delibera-tion. We set forth the grounds and necessity for such, realizing that church as well as society can become so polarized around social issues such as abortion (see chapter 8 here).

In developing guiding principles in a social statement on eco-nomic life,[2] those on the task force ranged from a venture capitalist to those entrapped in and addressing systemic poverty. Listening posts took us to persons involved in the federal government and on Wall Street, as well as those unemployed. The faith-grounded social statement with its rather progressive policy recommenda-tions was adopted by an ELCA church-wide assembly (1999) with hardly any changes, and has provided bases for many public ad-vocacy stances ever since. A number of other social statements on other critical topics have been developed and adopted since then, providing a basis for the ELCA to become a more public church.

These challenges were far greater in my subsequent call to direct the Department for Theology and Studies of the Lutheran

2. ELCA, "Sufficient, Sustainable Livelihoood for All."

World Federation (1999–2010), pursuing much of this work with ecumenical and interfaith partners. My intent was to encourage those in what has become the majority global South to examine critically the theology and practices they had inherited from missionaries, as well as the importance of those from much different contexts being able to listen, learn and be transformed through their interaction with one another. This climaxed in 2009 in what then was the largest gathering of Lutheran theologians, half of whom were from the global South. Along with a host of others, seeds were being planted in soil (the "culture" of church and society) that at that stage was still tightly packed, resistant to change, and not very inviting. Gradually as the ground would be loosened through God's Spirit, this soil would become more fertile, enabling the seeds to germinate and grow into mature plants.

Today woman are extensively and prominently present as spokespersons throughout American society. Yet women and other minorities end up in corporate leadership positions mainly in times of downturn or turmoil, which also applies to churches and seminaries. Advocacy still is needed especially by and for those of lower income, of color, and globally, where unjust gender and racist practices remain entrenched. Increasingly, in light of gender changes, attention to what it means to be male in society as well as globally has become more urgent. With lightning speed, the waves of changes in societies of the global North have swept over gay, lesbian, bisexual and transgender realities, but leaving many in the global South astounded and puzzled. As I was asked some years ago in Nigeria, why is it that the sexual and marriage ethic Northern missionaries taught Nigerians fifty years ago is now so changed? I ponder how struggles for greater gender equality can join with rather than perpetuating the various waves of imperialism that have dominated the world for so long.

I now realize that "seeing-remembering-connecting" were key practices in what I was doing continually through the many LWF consultations and publications. In staffing and editing such, I especially sought to make it possible for people to be present and voices to be heard that for too long had been silenced. This included making it possible for voices of African women to be heard, as they spoke and wrote for the first time of the abuses and injustices that they had experienced under patriarchal practices that had long kept them silent.

Forty years ago, "global" had a positive ring for me, but in recent years "globalization" has increasingly become suspect for many in the world, especially because of how neoliberal practices driving it have wreaked havoc on so many. This was a jarring realization for U.S. American seminarians when they interacted with church leaders from around the world in the annual January course we offered in Geneva. As one current pastor who participated in such remarked to me recently, "nothing has so transformed me and my ministry." "Trans-contextual," "transfigurational," and "transformational" became key words in the theological work I pursued through the LWF and in seminaries where I have taught.

In teaching at seminaries[3] as well as speaking in many other settings in this country and around the world, I have frequently noted some of the shortfalls indicated here in the first chapter. The theme of "faith active in love" is being lived out by many congregations, with considerable charitable outreach, but typically this stops short of challenging, much less changing unjust structural systemic realities. The church was and still is mostly reacting to what is occurring in society but seldom a noticed actor in public life.[4] The wider structural realities feel too overwhelming, leaving people feeling powerless to change such. Yet I continually recall what my mentor Dorothee Soelle had taught me: faith is a struggle against objective cynicism.

There continue to be significant gaps between what the church's official stances are and the ongoing practices of ordinary people, both within and outside the church. How can a

3. Lutheran School of Theology at Chicago, Wartburg Theological Seminary in Dubuque, Lutheran Theological Seminary at Philadelphia, School of Theology and Ministry at Seattle University, Waterloo Seminary at Wilfrid Laurier University (Canada), Pacific Lutheran Theological Seminary in Berkeley.

4. African-American churches have been a notable exception, currently inspired by the Black Lives Matter movement.

more intentional nurturing of "seeing-remembering-connecting" help bridge those gaps? How might attention to these three focal practices become means for drawing people more deeply into key theological insights and practices? How can these verbs or practices, nurtured over the long-term in and through communities of faith, lead more deeply into understandings and actions? How might these be subversive of the systemic injustices that pervade society, for the sake of bearing bolder witness to what God seeks and is doing in the world today? That is an intent of the chapters that follow.

Now with my husband, I have come full circle to the San Francisco Bay Area again, which is where some of the most significant "seeing-remembering-connecting" first began to occur for me. Portions of the following material have already been discussed in a number of classes I have taught, presentations I have made, and articles I have written. These chapters bring together in a more comprehensive and developed way, drawing selectively from what has previously been published in some of my recent articles.[5]

In bringing this together here, my hope is that this will provoke reflection on how common practices evoked by seeing-remembering-connecting might become bridges between those grounded in long-established teachings and practices of the faith and those who find such irrelevant.

In this book I summarize rather than extensively discussing the critical challenges we confront today. Through the years, many people and works have informed what is written here, some of which are selectively indicated here. To *all* who have affected what I write here, I am most grateful.

Rather than providing specific prescriptions for how to change churches (or other communities), my intent is to provide a framework that invites and inspires people to consider and discuss with others what this implies or calls for in specific situations. How

---

5. Bloomquist, "*Ekklesia* in the Midst of Moral Outrage Today"; "Transforming Domination Then and Now"; and "Subversive Practices of Being Church."

might this provoke new expressions and practices of what it means to be *ecclesia* in our world today?

Let the conversations, insights, and changes that this might stir up for you begin!

1

"Church in Society" Today?

- Why are churches in North America not more forthrightly speaking out and acting to transform today's blatant realities of injustice, illusion, and amnesia that fly in the face of the faith they confess?

- How are competing gods, faiths, and hopes at stake?

- How might churches become places where "subversions" of reality are nurtured and alternative public visions held forth and pursued by the people of God for the sake of the world?

These are some of the motivating questions for this book. This is not yet another attempt to decry or diagnose the decline or disillusionment with the church today, nor is it another litany of what is wrong with society, although it is builds on much that has been written in this regard. Nor does it intend to provide a set of "how to's" for reviving or renewing the local church to be relevant in its social context. There are many genres of books and articles and workshops that do that already, some with commonalities but also with some differences from what will be set forth here.

The approach here is more radical, going to the core of what the church is about (ecclesiology) and developing theological approaches and insights for how church, not so much as an institution fearing for its own survival, but as a dynamic *ecclesia* or movement might be lived out or practiced today. It draws some insights from what has been referred to as the emerging church movement but also from practices and traditions embodied in more traditional established churches. It draws from theological understandings of the Reformation but also is informed by ecumenical and interfaith impulses of our day.

In this inductive approach, the societal context, rather than doctrinal understandings, becomes the point of departure. This is not primarily a work in Christian social ethics, although it is permeated with these concerns. Instead, it insists that challenges in society need to be addressed *theologically*, and thus bear witness to the faith in increasingly secular and interfaith contexts. This contrasts with moving quickly to practical considerations of how "we can fix the problem" or "what works," short-term responses that usually do not address the actual structures and ideologies that perpetuate domination and injustice.

In the United States, as well as in much of the "developed" world, the church increasingly is not the respected and influential player in society as it has been previously. Historic mainline churches are decreasing in size and influence. Non-denominational community churches may be growing, in some cases dramatically compared to established churches, but typically in ways that serve as a shelter, escape, or relief from all that "bad stuff" going on in society, rather than engaging and working to transform what is unjust. To do so is considered too overwhelming, potentially controversial, or even divisive in many settings, including in congregations affiliated with denominations where social justice commitments have been assumed to be strong.

As they have since the time of the early church, many do actively live out their faith, through spontaneous as well as organized actions of compassion toward those who are vulnerable or with particular material, emotional, and spiritual needs. "Faith active in love" and "God's work, our hands" are themes that have caught on and *are* being lived out. But typically these efforts stop short of critiquing and working to change ideologies, dynamics and structures that perpetuate the injustices and continue escalating the needs.

I stand with those who maintain that justice is central to a faith grounded in the Bible and who decry what has happened to the more prophetic voice and stance of faith communities of a generation or so ago, when they were prominent in the Civil Rights and anti-apartheid movements. Many wonder what has happened to the prophetic nerve of the church, as inspired by the prophets, by how Jesus expressed and lived out alternatives to the dominant assumptions and ruling practices of his day, and how reformers such as Martin Luther spoke out in stark terms against the banking and other powers of his day (see chapter 3).

The church failing to "speak truth to power" is one reason why so many are leaving or becoming disillusioned with the institutional church. It has lost its nerve and no longer "walks the talk," no longer lives out the radical resistance to and transformation of unjust realities, which is at the heart of the biblical witness.

Much that in the past has been written and taught in courses on "church in society," particularly in U.S. settings, has assumed a strong church and a relatively stable society.[1] Faith communities have been viewed in terms of their ability to influence and shape society, and in some times and places they *have* done that. Certainly African-American churches have played important roles in this regard. But for the most part, mainline white churches have reflected or legitimatized society's values and power interests.

Churches in North America have typically

- been upholders or legitimizers of American values and of culture Christianity;

- promoted church growth and effective marketing of the church;

- emphasized maintenance rather than mission;

---

1. For example, these were the mid-20th century assumptions in the much used typology of H. Richard Niebuhr in *Christ and Culture*. Having taught "church in society" for many years in different settings I am increasingly aware of the inadequacies of these and others approaches, which is why I am developing a different approach here.

- compassionately reached out to assist people who are vulnerable or in need but not focused on changing policies or structures that keep them in need;

- lived out the faith (discipleship) mostly in relation to what is close by and familiar—personal life, family, work, one's immediate community;

- avoided what might be controversial or threatening to vested power interests.

Some have emphasized the theological substance needed today, such as a theology of grace in the midst of a society based on works righteousness. Others have emphasized just *being* the church—without worrying about its public social witness in the world. Faithful preaching of the Word and celebration of the sacraments is what matters, and it *does,* even if among a faithful remnant in a shrinking church. But there is great caution or reluctance to make connections that will challenge or change what is going on in social contexts. After all, fearful, shrinking churches cannot afford to lose any more of their faithful remnant who might disagree.

Overall, insufficient attention has been given to how values, assumptions, and ways of operating as churches may themselves be reflective of the very domination or "empire" that itself needs to be challenged theologically—in other words, from out of the heart of the church's beliefs and practices.

> The global market's most insidious impact on the life of the church appears in theology, organizational life, liturgy and worship, and spirituality. In response to the demands of "church shoppers," the church's primary identity has been transformed into a vendor of individual salvation or a service provider . . . and less a community with a distinct identity experiencing God's transforming power and seeking to transform the world.[2]

A shortfall of approaches that begin with the individual is that they tend to stay there and seldom lead to actual transformation

2. Fernandez, "Church as a Household," 175.

4

in the social-economic-political arena, of structural realities of injustice "out there," which also infect personal life. There may be passing awareness and lamenting about these injustices, but not much effective coming together of individuals to actually change what are perceived as realities external to the life of faith.

For North Americans, beginning with the world is strategic because of how this subverts our usual tendency to focus on ourselves, on a private, spiritual realm as a refuge (or fortress) from "all the bad stuff out there." The usual sequence is that we are fed, inspired, get ourselves together and then go out, sharing what we have for the sake of others. Preferably we do so corporately, as the body of Christ in society, not just as individuals. But still the shortfall of this is that we often don't seem to get it together enough (our internal acts as the church) to getting around to the "going out" dimensions. The focus is on ourselves (those already in the church) rather than on an enlarged sense of "us," which focusing on the world brings in *from the beginning*. In other words, churches tend to have an internally- rather than externally-oriented identity. We stay focused on ourselves (those in church), rather than externally-oriented identity, that a focus on *the world* in all its diversity brings in from the beginning.

U.S Christians tend to focus on what we should *do* to "help" others, whether close at hand or globally. The activist mode typical of Americans is that, upon hearing of injustices, our immediate response is: "What can we do for them?" This usually is based on a contrast between *our* richness/affluence and *their* neediness or deficiencies. There are lots of crucial ways in which basic human needs are served in this way. Yet the power relations, and the structures/policies that reinforce them, remain in place in such an "us vs. them" manner. What are we going to do *for them* might be done in an accompanying mode—doing "with" rather than doing "for." But usually this stops short of reflecting on how the *relationship or structure of power* between "them and us" needs to be reconsidered and transformed. Through *communio* relationships, empowered through the Spirit of God, giver and receiver are both transformed. Justice involves changing the relations that link us together.

At the same time, "An exclusive wide-angle view on structures is just as much of an oversimplification as an exclusive narrow focus on individuals . . . it compromises our ability to find adequate solutions to real world problems. Avoiding the particular also blinds us to our real allies when they are right in front of us."[3]

What happens spiritually to the individual really *does* matter, but the vague hope is that transformed individuals will somehow make a difference in society. Individuals can and do make a difference, but this typically stops short of intentional, organized efforts at social change. Why is this? The ability or capacity for impacting wider structures and policies usually feels too overwhelming. Even when we come together with others, we feel powerless in the face of such. Yet succumbing to this is itself a basic faith or confessional matter.

Church leaders fear that publicly speaking and working for systemic change will lead to controversy, because we don't know how to disagree and seek common ground. In an individualistic culture, individual opinions hold sway, rather than the communal values rooted in Scripture and intrinsic to the common good.

The few churches who intentionally seek to be more prophetic, *do* take on issues or causes where injustice is especially blatant, particularly when they have a personal connection with such. Often this occurs in sporadic spurts of crying out, even with public outrage, but which may not be effective in the longer term work of actually changing the structures or policies at stake. This prophetic denunciation often rises up or is heard in ways that may alienate members or established interests in society and church. At least that is the *fear* of what will happen. When these voices rise up, or even threaten to do so, pastors and other church leaders tend to shut down. When a church feels weak or unstable already, it tends to be vulnerable to reactions, and thus retreats back into ever more privatized expressions of church. Ironically, in this way attempts to become a more public church can instead result in a more privatized preoccupation.

3. DeChristopher, "The Value of Protest," par. 9. This refers to interruptions by Black Lives Matter leaders at candidates' rallies.

In recent years, there have been increasing emphases on the public church (in contrast to churches being primarily focused on the private realm) with an array of notable efforts to put this into effect. Many more advocacy organizations and movements for social justice have sprung up, and regularly appeal for support. These have been crucial for members of faith communities to come together with others in order effectively to impact political and economic developments and policies, especially by collaborating ecumenically and with those of other faiths. Intentional efforts are even made for congregations to become "advocating congregations," publicly embracing this as part of their mission, or to become part of other movements and organizations pursuing social or environmental justice. But realistically in most congregations, these intentional involvements tend to be pursued by only a small number of special interest members, committees, or task forces, who continually express frustration that not more are involved. Others are glad that such organizations are carrying out this work but hesitate getting more involved because of the political differences this could ignite. This could become a diversion from what *they* consider the central calling of the church—to serve the spiritual needs of its members—rather than seeing these wider pursuits of justice as central to what the church is called to be about.

The wider structural injustices—such as those that lead to greater economic inequalities—may lie behind some of the individual pathologies regularly encountered in pastoral care. Mental illnesses are three times as common in developed countries where there are bigger income gaps between rich and poor. Conditions such as mania and narcissism are related to striving for status and dominance, while disorders such as anxiety and depression may involve responses to continual experiences of subordination. "The data all point to the fact that as larger differences in material circumstances create greater social distances, feelings of superiority and inferiority increase. In short, growing inequality makes us all more neurotic about 'image management' and how we are seen by others."[4]

4. Wilkinson and Pickett, "How Inequality," par. 1–3.

New expressions of church, often loosely a part of the "emerging church" movement, are sometimes begun with the express purpose of addressing certain social, economic, or environmental injustices and unpacking understandings of the faith in relation to such. These may appeal to those who have been disillusioned or turned off by established churches and who are unlikely to join these churches. But what occurs in and through these new expressions of church often remains separate from what is happening in more established congregations. These are accused (often falsely) of being boring and root-bound to historic traditions and practices, to how things always have been done, and detached from— rather than really engaging—what is occurring around them in the world today.

Transformation for the Sake of the World

Are there possibilities for re-conceiving what faith communities are and can be about? How can the nurture and effective resistance to structural realities of injustice be more deeply and explicitly embedded throughout ongoing faith formation and practices? How then might "church in society" be understood and approached differently than in the late twentieth and early twenty-first century? How might this be expressed in more socially transformative ways, through theological education but also in ways that can connect with those without formal theological training or who may not even identify themselves as "Christian"?

Instead of first asking how established churches might or already are affecting, impacting or changing the societal problems around them, here the focus begins with deeper analyses of the reigning ideologies, dynamics and structures that hold people in bondage, and how to engage *this* theologically. This approach is consistent with Martin Luther's approach, already back in the sixteenth century. Basic faith questions arise out of our being embedded in what is going on in our society, and in the natural and human-made world of which we are a part, rather than primarily through individual spiritual quests that are the popular trend in our day.

In what follows, this will be probed through three focal verbs or linked practices: seeing–remembering–connecting. These reflect what the church in its basic practices and orientations has long been about, which subsequent chapters will delve into more deeply. In a generic sense these practices are also shared in common and can be a bridge with those who stand outside faith communities, bridging secular and sacred life realms and the words distinctive to them. These are starting points that are more readily understandable and accessible to those outside churches. They are also verbs intended to engage and counter crucial systemic matters plaguing societies today, as manifested, for example, in illusions, amnesia and individualism. Furthermore, they are re-envisioned as key practices through which divinely-empowered social transformation of realities of injustice and domination can and does occur, in ways that are simultaneously deeply pastoral and prophetic.

Seeing–remembering–connecting permeates the heart of what theological practice is about—not theology as abstract or theoretical but living, embodied, real. These ordinary practices become extraordinary when viewed through theological lenses. God is revealing, remembering, and connecting, becoming manifest in and through what these verbs imply, but always as far more than what we can grasp, comprehend, or realize—in other words, as transcendentally immanent.

We glimpse or get a sense of what God is about in our lives and world through seeing–remembering–connecting. We begin to see, remember, connect what we would not otherwise, and to do so collaboratively, for the sake of the world. The church is in and for the sake of the world because it sees, remembers, and connects *theologically*. It is one holy apostolic and catholic, a gift of God that comes from beyond realities on the ground, thus transforming all that is in light of what has been (remembering the past) and is to be (envisioning the future). We see, remember, and connect with another reality that not only is possible but becoming manifest here and now.

9

2

A Subversive Church of the Cross

Subversive today?

"Subversive" is not how most of those associated with churches to-day would view themselves. In most countries of the North, and in many of the South, churches are viewed as upholders of the social order with its values and assumptions. For example, about half of U.S. Americans, when recently surveyed, think of theirs as being a "Christian" nation, and indeed such symbols are embedded in the political culture in many ways. But this was not emphasized until the 1930s, when key business leaders "inspired a public relations offensive that cast capitalism as the handmaiden of Christianity." They also recruited key clergy to join their cause. For example, "the Rev. James W. Fifield—known as 'the 13th Apostle of Big Business' and 'Saint Paul of the Prosperous'—dismissed New Testament warnings about the corrupting nature of wealth, and . . . paired Christianity and capitalism against the New Deal's 'pagan statism.'"[1]

Although this usually is more subtle today, there still is the expectation that churches and church leaders will support rather than critique the established order, with its assumptions, values, and practices. That contributed to the upsurge in U.S. church

1. Kruse, "A Christian Nation?" par . 9.

growth in the 1950s. Some today yearn to return to that time when churches were growing and "successful." Corporate business practices and ways of operating increasingly rule today. Pastors of congregations and leaders of church-related organizations who do not go along with this continuing expectation for "success" and its associated values and practices are dismissed, silenced, or at least threatened with funding cutbacks. Of course, this is nothing new for many churches around the world, where being identified as a Christian long has been considered subversive, leading to ostracism, persecution, and even death.

An increasing number of people today are disillusioned with, disaffiliate from, or refuse to join such established expressions of church and the economic, political, and cultural forces to which they have become captive. They wonder, Why are churches not more forthrightly speaking out and acting to transform today's realities of domination—the injustices, illusions, and empire—that fly in the face of the faith Christians confess? How might churches become places where "subversions" of reality can be nurtured and alternative public visions held forth and pursued, for the sake of the world?

Increasingly, biblical scholars view Christianity's historical origins as being determined to resist the idolatry and power of the Roman empire.[2] Jesus' teachings and ministry in Galilee evoked "a powerful communal response to the very real conditions of poverty and oppression."[3] Later, as the church became more established under Christendom and increasingly a collaborator with the political powers, this subversive witness faded.

Walter Brueggemann refers to Scripture as a "sub-version," a rendering of reality that lives under the dominant version, a dominant imagination that screens out all other neighbors, who can be screened out if the God of all Neighborliness is fashioned instead as a God who celebrates individual achievement.[4] Subversion is a dimension of neighbor-love for all people and creation. The

2. Horsley and Silberman, *The Message*, 232.

3. Ibid, 93.

4. Brueggemann, *Word Militant*, 152.

11

courage to embody it is born of love; it arises from the indwelling of Christ within believers. "Subversive moral agency undermines domination and injustice, forging more faithful ways of life."[5] This includes resistance but also re-visioning and rebuilding.

The typical practices of the church usually are not considered to be subversive. Yet when pursued more deeply in societies where neoliberal assumptions, practices, and expected outcomes prevail, the common ordinary practices intrinsic in being church are bound to lead in directions that go against the grain, challenge, and thus are seen as subversive of the status quo. We may not set out to be "subversive" but living out the heart of the faith we confess is likely to lead there. When it does, we are tempted to draw back, adapt so as to become more acceptable, so as not to upset the vested interest of the powers that rule. But in submitting to such fears, we end up denying the faith we claim to confess.

To begin naming what we are up against signals that confessing faith in this kind of God clearly can be dangerous or at least risky. The words are effective; they provoke reactions. To confess and live out faith in the Triune God can be risky, especially when society and government are captive to economic and geopolitical interests, and strike out at those who threaten these interests. Yet "[t]he one narrated and revealed between Good Friday and Pentecost as God's own Son constitutes the revolutionary *subversion* of all human thought and expectation, embodying the utter contrast between God's kingdom and ours."[6]

I propose that the practice of "subversive remembering" is a crucial power discourse in the midst of systemic injustices, social amnesia and illusions. It is a subversive declaration of who and whose we are in the midst of those forces that would dominate, oppress, and shape us according to their power and interests. More than only words, this becomes a stance of defiance in the face of these realities. It is inevitably contextual and political. It emerges from beyond what is, as an effective power that activates us with new life, and gathers us together as the body of Christ, empowered

5. Moe-Lobeda, *Healing a Broken World*, 13.

6. Lewis, *Between Cross and Resurrection*, 310; emphasis added.

to cooperate and organize with others to resist these powers reigning over us and making us feel powerless.

The church as the body of Christ is called to embody and live this out, in testimony to the incarnation. The incarnation, in which God in Christ pitched his tent among us, is God's supreme "occupation." This occurs in the midst of impoverishment, downturn, and death, which is *not* where we expect to find God. Rather than reinforcing the privilege of the powerful, and symbolized accordingly, God is with those who matter little in the eyes of the world, those who are poor, excluded, and victimized. They are liberated for new life in just, participatory communities that here are characterized by the linked practices of seeing–remembering–connecting.

"How can the church participate in the divine fellowship of God [the Triune God] without also sharing in God's own participation in the world's suffering, forsakenness and death?"[7] This is made real or incarnate through practices such as care, accompaniment, hospitality, advocacy, and community-building, even among those who may not share Christian convictions. Our faith makes us open to life as lived by others, as exemplified in how Jesus related to all kinds of people, without regard for their religious background. Rather than "lording" faith over others in attempts to convert them, the true meaning of what we confess and live out should be how it embraces and transforms human suffering.

For the Sake of the World

I propose that the theological starting point is in the world; what is going on there becomes a "wake up" call to the church. The world is "in our face" as a church because the world is very much "in" us. The real faith struggles of our day are not necessarily with other recognizable faiths (Islam, etc.), but with the unquestioned ideologies that reign over and distort our lives. Churches that assume they are set apart from the world often operate with assumptions and practices that actually are more affected or shaped by the

7. Ibid., 346.

ideologies and practices reigning in their world or culture than they are by biblical/theological perspectives—particularly in their quest to be "successful." It is not that the world tells the church how to be the church, but the world opens up challenges that the church must engage if it is to be faithful, a bearer of news that actually is "good" today—liberating, healing, transforming what holds us and all of creation in bondage.

"For the sake of the world" may seem like a significant shift from how sixteenth-century reforming movements tended to be preoccupied with the church and salvation, rather than with what was going on in the world. The signing in 1999 of the Joint Declaration on the Doctrine of Justification by the Catholic and Lutheran churches was celebrated as an ecumenical milestone, and indeed it was; *oecumene*, however, has to do not only with the church, but with the whole world. Here, where people's many kinds of bondage, fears, and hopes are focused today is where these central theological insights of the Reformation have hardly begun to penetrate.

If Reformation insights are to have an enduring, living significance in the world today—a world of massive injustice, illusions, and bankrupt hopes—then its theological insights must be able to communicate not only with those within the church, but more importantly for the sake of *this world* that God so loves. What new possibilities might this open up for how the faith can be embodied and conveyed, especially among those who are skeptical as to whether the church has anything worthwhile to offer the world today?

Toward a subversive ecclesia crucis

Guillermo Hansen provocatively suggests how a "Lutheran theological code" might become transformative of the challenges we face in today's world. This code includes how the cross (dis) locates the sacred into the realm of the profane—into the world. The cross is a subversive code that challenges all cultural and religious notions of what is considering transcendent or successful in life.[8] It is where our current ways of knowing are questioned and destabilized, making room for what is truly new and different. It is a verdict that something is fundamentally wrong with how the world is structured.[9] The cross interrogates and destabilizes what is generally known, thus opening up space for what is truly new and different. The cross appears as the center of a new gospel, as a sociopolitical event. Furthermore, the God who transcends ("falls") into our world, justifies the victims of imperial power,[10] radically redrawing the boundaries of God's domain to include those considered outcasts. "God's twofold rule is for the sake of a public theology, to bring forth worlds in which people can live, through radical democracy as a living alternative through the networks spawned by empire."[11]

The church living by a theology of the cross is taken more fully and deeply into the world. This key emphasis in Luther's theology needs to be pursued, for the sake of forming an *ecclesia* that is transformative—even subversive—of the injustice, empire, and domination of many kinds that hold the world captive today. Alan Lewis provocatively asks whether "we who speak and preach so glibly about Christ crucified and cutely carry round our necks and on our vestments symbols of this death and burial are truly ready to push the churches we belong to on that costly way of the cross toward institutional and denominational *kenosis*, for the sake of our speedily disintegrating world."[12]

The vantage point of the cross, along with a collective sense of the structural sin in which we are complicit, brings a critique that should be undergone, thereby exposing vulnerability and fallibility. Thus, we must engage in practices to "see in truthful ways," so that the knowing might become "compelling," so that we might "glimpse the presence of God and the holiness of the church in

8. Hansen, "Resistance, Adaptation, or Challenge,"30.

9. Ibid., 31.

10. Ibid., 32.

11. Ibid., 35.

12. Lewis, *Between Cross and Resurrection*, 393.

15

unlikely places."[13] Sites of vulnerability are privileged; they are where God can be seen more truly.

An epistemology (way of knowing) through the cross becomes especially crucial when illusions fall apart, when they no longer hold. We begin to see what really is going on, understand our implications in it, and accept our accountability to act accordingly. The cross is the fulcrum for knowing; it is the hinge point of true reality and the gift to see it.[14] To know truly is to know from the margins of life, sanity, dignity, power. Friends of the cross are those who "live in the world as it is, without illusions."[15] "The church of the cross becomes a visible alternative to the ways of the world *in and through* its immersion in it."[16]

In deeply encountering persons and realities far different from our own—in relocating ourselves—our complicity with injustice is exposed. Building on these understandings and practices distinctive to a church that is porously and intentionally open to the world, this can nurture and lead toward transformation of what today is holding people in bondage, ideologically, and practically.

13. Mahn, "What are Churches *For?*" 18–19.
14. Solberg, *Compelling Knowledge,* 90.
15. Ibid., 83.
16. Mahn, 21.

3

How Luther Challenged Dominating Power in His Day

The theological crisis in the sixteenth century

In Martin Luther's time, the Papacy had become the most powerful institution ruling over people's lives, with closely intertwined religious, social, cultural, and political aspects. Under this system, no one could do enough so as to be certain of his/her salvation. Luther came to view this institutional power of domination as a theological matter threatening salvation itself.[1] His theological critique of this domination, which he raised out a pastoral concern for people's salvation, became the means through which Luther began to break through the whole Roman system of domination.

Luther broke open the system of domination in his day, by proposing a much different relationship with God. He responded both to people's fears and captivity connected with their social longings (their desires) *and* touched the ecclesial nerve center: its financial support and its divine legitimacy.[2] Luther wanted to find a crack/crisis in the reigning consensus of church, economy, and politics, by cracking the surface. The justice of God breaks in and

---

1. Hendrix, *Luther and the Papacy*, xii.
2. Altmann, "Justification," 121.

fragments the systems of the world.[3] The theology of the cross frees theology from captivity to the dominant modes of rationality.

Justification by grace overcomes in principle and in practice the division between religious and secular aspects of life in the medieval world. God's justification causes us to see ourselves, our neighbor, and the world differently, not based on inherent acceptability or net worth, but in ways that are counter-cultural, even subversive of the reigning ideologies. "Justification is prophetic speech from the heart of the divine pathos . . . a call to remembrance that is deeper than morality or civility."[4] It is transcendent beyond any promise of the reigning structural or ideological bondage. "Justification is God's mission of love for the world."[5]

A pervasive thread running throughout Luther's writings was his intent to make this breakthrough practical, experiential, and accessible to common ordinary folk in the struggles they face. He seemed aware of the need to deal with both the objective and subjective realities of what was holding people in bondage in his time. Rather than primarily mounting a frontal attack on the institution holding people captive then, he attacked the actual practices that played into and supported the reigning system of domination. He did this on deeply theological grounds. Luther boldly declared that through the preaching of faith, centered especially in the doctrine of justification, practices such "indulgences, purgatory, vows, Masses, and similar abominations come tumbling down, taking with them the ruin of the entire papacy . . . solely by the Spirit."[6]

For Luther, the subjective or internal reality of God's justification/salvation has objective or external consequences. Both theology and economy are at stake, which is why Luther attacked both indulgences and usury.[7] If justification remains confined to a spiritual realm apart from societal implications, or in distinction from the critical relational dimensions of *communio* that

3. Westhelle, *Scandalous God,* 41.

4. Tiede, "Justifying faith," 113.

5. Ibid., 119.

6. Luther, "Lectures on Galatians —1535," in *Luther's Works,* 26: 221, 223.

7. Westhelle, *Scandalous God,* 47.

flow from it, then injustices will continue to have free reign. These distort our most basic relationships to God, ourselves, and one another. This is not to imply that the world can be governed by the gospel; we need to resist any such theocracy tendencies. But what is unleashed is a power that cannot remain quiet or passive in the face of unjust systems, because of how they themselves distort theological anthropology and hold people in captivity both spiritually and materially. In this sense, justification and justice are intimately connected.[8]

The Eucharist Distorted

One focus of Luther's protest against the domination reigning in his day, was how the sacraments (especially Holy Communion) were being used by the Roman church for power and control over the people, and thus distorted as God's gift of grace and freedom "The Eucharist became a locus where the Church could exercise its control over the sacred . . . the mystery itself . . . instrumentalized."[9]

By the middle of the twelfth century, the church was eager to assert the real presence of the human and the divine Christ against various spiritualizing challenges, and began to refer to the host as the *corpus Christi* (the body of Christ). The term for the host, *corpus mysticum,* was gradually transferred to the church. Rather than the church referred to as the body of Christ (*corpus Christi*), the host in the Eucharist was referred to as such.

In this context, the Eucharist was given a strategic function: to consolidate the church, by positing not just the equivalence but the identity between a mystical reality and the visible, and by making that depend upon hierarchical authority. Hence, it became a

8. I recall how the Reformed churches (WARC) refrained from sign onto the Joint Declaration on the Doctrine of Justification until the connections between justification and justice were made more explicit. Although Lutherans had pursued that earlier, especially with regard to Latin American realities of injustice, this was not further pursued in theological work underlying the official Lutheran/Catholic dialogues regarding justification.

9. Schwartz, *Sacramental Poetics,* 20

miracle made possible through the power of the church—a power seemingly prior to the miracle. In this way, the Eucharist became a locus where the church could exercise its control over the sacred.

> This co-optation of the Eucharist also vastly accentuated the institution's hierarchy, formalism and legalism . . . There is a profound difference between a hierarchical institution appropriating salvific power and the much earlier Christian belief that the Eucharist itself has the sacramental power to create a healthy social body. Mystery is the domain beyond human control but here *sacramentality* is no longer contrasted to *instrumentality* for the mystery itself has been instrumentalized.[10]

The Reformation occurred at the beginning of modernism and the birth of the modern self, with the subsequent dominations to which this led: "the figure of the Other is gradually replaced by the Self who defines and controls all he [sic] sways."[11] Instead, the intention of the Eucharist is "to create a community that coheres not through particular identities" but through "the potential of reconciliation harbored by communion to inspire a world of community,"[12] based on God's justice and compassion for all.

Luther confronts the emerging capitalist practices of his time

Luther had widespread pastoral and ethical concern for those affected negatively by economic matters, which was reflected extensively in his writings and counsel. He called on Christians to exercise neighbor-love or charity to those in need, both through individual and governmental means (e.g., the "common chest," an early version of government social welfare). Economic matters should not remain autonomous or in a sphere apart from spiritual matters. When they threaten to become a power of domination

10. Ibid.
11. Ibid., 139.
12. Ibid., 141.

ruling over people—as was occurring through the early capitalist practices of Luther's time—then they become a spiritual matter of idolatry (an idol being whatever we trust in instead of God).

There is a sense in which Luther was fighting both against the ascetic drive from money, as in the prevailing spirituality of his day, and against the acquisitive drive for it, as in the emerging capitalism of his day.[13] For Luther, neither was salvific, but directly conflicted with the theological core of justification. His attack on works-righteousness was also an attack on the early profit economy. Rather than money being used to make more money, it should remain as God's gift for serving the neighbor and building community.

Luther viewed early capitalism as beginning to function as a domination structure.[14] Its practices were devouring the poor. "The world was becoming one big whorehouse where the big thieves hang the little thieves."[15] According to Luther, the power of trading companies manipulated people's minds and veiled the truth, so that capital formation through charging high interest was seen as good. "So sweet is the poison of the paradise apple that they want to make Mammon their god and raise themselves through his power to become gods over poor, lost and miserable people."[16] Usurers and idolaters serve Mammon; they lack credibility, and "cannot have or receive the forgiveness of sins, nor the grace of Christ, nor the communion of saints."[17] In other words, they should be excommunicated.

In his explanation of the Seventh Commandment, Luther wrote that stealing is "taking advantage of someone . . . wherever business is transacted and money is exchanged for good or services"[18] "Thieves . . . sit in their chairs and are known as great

13. Lindberg, "Luther on Poverty," 149.

14. Chung, *Church*, 41.

15. *Luther's Works*, 21:180.

16. Chung, et al, *Liberating Lutheran Theology*, 177 (their translation of Luther's "Admonition to Clergy").

17. Ibid., 178.

18. "Large Catechism," in Kolb and Wengert, *Book of Concord*, 416.

lords and honorable, upstanding citizens, while they rob and steal under the cloak of legality. . . . the great, powerful archthieves *with whom lords and princes consort* [italics in original] and who daily plunder not just a city or two, but all of Germany."[19]

Luther accused the Catholic church of protecting such thieves. Spiritual governance was geared toward what would make money (the selling of indulgences is but one example). As reflected in a number of his writings, Luther clearly sensed the political-economic alliance—the interlocking powers of domination—that was developing between the Catholic church, the reigning government (i.e., Charles V), and emerging large economic powers (e.g., the Fuggers).[20]

The problem was not only how greedy individual were using money but the structural social damage inherent in the idolatry of the "law" of the market, which was impersonal and autonomous. The rising world economy was already beginning to suck up urban and local economies, and increasing gaps between the rich and the poor. This can destroy the ethos of the community. This is why Luther considered this systematic matter to be a *status confessionis* (matter of faith not just ethics).[21]

Building on this today

Consistent with Luther, in a 2012 public statement of the Lutheran World Federation (LWF), this systemic domination was assessed in terms of the ancient vice of greed:

> While greed has been prevalent throughout human history, under modern neoliberal capitalism, the virus of insatiability (never having enough) has turned into a general epidemic [and leading to ever greater economic disparities]. Greed has become systemic—built into the reigning reality that is accepted as inevitable. This becomes similar to the domination or bondage of sin, as

19. Ibid., 417.
20. Chung, *Church*, 39.
21. Lindberg, "Luther on Poverty, 148.

expressed through the theology of Paul (e.g., Romans 6) and Luther. It becomes the idol, for which lives, communities and the rest of creation are sacrificed. Money and financial markets take on a life of their own. . . . More than just a medium of exchange, money has become a commodity from which ever larger profits are promised and expected.[22]

From Luther's theological perspective, when human constructs claim ultimacy for this life or beyond, God's righteousness denounces them as idols and displaces them with the justification received through faith.[23] "When the accumulation of power and wealth become totalitarian, as in the Hellenistic-Roman Empire, the only way for faithful Jews and followers of the Messiah Jesus to react is resistance and defiance."[24] The totality of this system can only be critiqued or de-idolatrized via an equally encompassing claim on our lives, i.e., the God made known to us in Jesus Christ, as discerned and lived out in community with one another.

Thus, as the 2003 LWF Assembly declared:

As a communion, we must engage the false ideology of neoliberal economic globalization . . . [which is] grounded in the assumption that the market, built on private property, unrestrained competition and the centrality of contracts, is the absolute law governing human life, society and the natural environment. This is idolatry and leads to the systematic exclusion of those who own no property, the destruction of cultural diversity, the dismantling of fragile democracies and the destruction of the earth.[25]

A year later (2004) in its Accra Confession, the World Alliance of Reformed Churches (WARC, now World Communion of Reformed Churches) declared this to be a matter of confession:

---

22. LWF, "Daily Bread Instead of Greed," 4.

23. Tiede, "Justifying Faith," 108.

24. Chung, et al, *Liberating*, 171.

25. LWF, "Daily Bread Instead of Greed," 1.

Therefore, we reject the current world economic order imposed by global neoliberal capitalism and any other economic system, including absolute planned economies, which defy God's covenant by excluding the poor, the vulnerable and the whole of creation from the fullness of life. We reject any claim of economic, political, and military empire which subverts God's sovereignty over life and acts contrary to God's just rule. . . . [and] the unregulated accumulation of wealth and limitless growth that has killed millions and destroyed much of God's creation.[26]

The global Radicalizing Reformation project seeks to bring these perspectives to the crises we face today. As stated in the preface to its theses:

The rampant destruction of human and non-human life in a world ruled by the totalitarian dictatorship of money and greed, market and exploitation requires a radical re-orientation towards the biblical message, which also marked the beginning of the Reformation. The dominant economic system and its imperial structures and policies have put the earth, human communities, and the future of our children up for sale. Our churches, congregations, and individual Christians have often become complacent and complicit with the established *status quo* and have lost their critical-prophetic power to protest, resist, and change what is occurring. God's justification by grace has been detached from social justice and thus serves as "useless salt" (Matt 5:13). Because the Reformation legacy has gone astray, we must at the same time return to some of Luther's thought and legacy, as well as standing decidedly against other things he said and did, if this is to become a *kairotic* time of transformation today.[27]

---

26. "Accra Confession," par. 19.

27._"Radicalizing Reformation—Provoked by the Bible and Today's Crises," preface.

4

Theologically Engaging Domination Today

> In the sixteenth century, the crisis was over the gospel
> that frees people from the fear and bondage of sin, which
> became embedded in systems needing to be challenged.
> Today, people also are in fear and bondage—over the sin
> of greed, as embedded in the economic system. They fear
> what the future will hold, unless dramatic changes are
> made for the sake of global economic and environmental
> justice. . . . Systemic greed becomes like the domination
> or bondage of sin that is expressed through the theology
> of Paul (e.g., Romans 6) and Luther.[1]

New awareness of this state of bondage has continued to grow and
become more obvious, but usually in ways that churches have not
dealt with on explicitly theological grounds. People today are feeling acutely betrayed by the promises they have bought into, often
with blind faith that now is increasingly feeling betrayed, e.g., by
large corporate interests determined to keep the market as "free" as
possible. Matters of basic meaning, hope and values were at stake
at the time of the Reformation, as well as today. But there have
been significant shifts in where that salvific hope is lodged.

1. LWF, "Daily Bread Instead of Greed," 3.

Systemic domination as "empire"

"Empire" refers to the various interrelated processes of domination and their effects, or as Joerg Rieger puts it, "massive concentrations of power which permeate all aspects of life and which cannot be controlled by any one actor alone."[2] Domination or power over more and more aspects of life is a characteristic of empire that causes, legitimates and exasperates injustices not only in our time but throughout history. What emerges under the category of "empire" is not just one kind of injustice but a complex of injustices, and how they are inter-related—economic, political, military, cultural, environmental, etc. Empire progressively incorporates the entire world within its open, expanding borders.

Four of the neoliberal tenets upholding empire today are that (1) economic growth will benefit all, (2) market freedom is the freedom that matters, (3) human beings are basically consumers rather than beings-in-community, and (4) corporate- and finance-driven economic globalization is inevitable.[3] Not only the realm of economic life but increasingly all arenas of life conform to this, including religious institutions if they are to survive economically. Neoliberalism has come to function like an idol; there is no choice but to submit, without critique. This is not only a moral matter, but a deeply theological matter of faith.

In short, "empire" counts loss as simply the cost of doing business, wants any grief to be voiced quietly and be over with, dismisses hope as fantasy, gives assurances of security and wellbeing that ring false, and provides absolute answers that cannot be contested, negotiated, or alternatives imagined.

Those preaching and teaching may have done the historical critical work and know the realities of empire against which biblical texts were written, but then they tend to stop short of helping people to see how this applies to the realities of empire as people actually experience them today. Opening this up so that people can see what is occurring in the world becomes as critical as good

2. Bloomquist, *Being the Church*, 13.

3. Moe-Lobeda, *Healing a Broken World*, 48–61.

exegesis of the biblical texts. This involves ongoing social, cultural, economic, political analyses that get at what is actually going on today. This becomes the point of theological engagement, so that the gospel breaks in as news that is "good," redemptive and transformative of the actual reigning realities that disrupt and destroy the world in which we and all of creation live today.

The readily identifiable empires and the highly objectionable violence and oppressions they have and continue to generate may be obvious, such as blatantly setting out to conquer people and cultures. Yet the more subtle ways in which empire operates, as a logic and set of practices that ensnare and enslave, often in unconscious ways that we do not see or recognize, are what especially is disturbing (e.g., the prison industrial complex and systemic racism). Current structures of empire are more all-encompassing than anything that has gone before, not only in terms of their geographical reach and ability to enforce order, but also in their ability to reach into and redefine cultural and even personal spheres. In this sense, resistance is difficult since most people never realize what it is that shapes them.

For example, high tech companies claim that they are granting people around the world "the power to share," which sounds like a universal social good, but the ever-new technologies they create are embedded with certain values, and intended to gain ever more customers, and thus be profitable. "In old fashioned 19th century imperialism, the Christian evangelists made a pretense of travelling separately from the conquering colonial forces. But in digital imperialism, everything travels as one, in the form of splendid technology itself: salvation and empire, missionary and magistrate, Bible and gun."[4]

Embedded in empire are systemic realities of injustice, going beyond what any one person does or fails to do. In this sense they are akin to the domination of sin that St. Paul discusses in his Epistle to the Romans, as well as the "powers and principalities" referred to in various places in the Bible. The powers and principalities leave individuals feeling powerless to do much that will be

4. Wasik, "Welcome to the Age of Digital Imperialism," par. 10.

effective in changing what is oppressing them. The reigning reality is all controlling, and seems far beyond human control, even when originally generated by humans. This is what poses the overarching theological challenge.

Exposing the idolatry is not simply a matter of denouncing, or taking a confessional stance against it, and attempting to extricate ourselves from it. We are too enmeshed in its complexities and compensations for that to be persuasive. We may not be "of it", but we are not immune from it. Nor can this lapse into other-worldly escapism. An objective naming of the idols, without engaging and subsequently transforming both the subjective and objective aspects of this domination, is not likely to lead to change. How can I disassociate from these powers on which I seem to depend for my sense of worth and future? What is needed is a theologically-inspired, critical engagement with the ideology legitimizing and increasing the disparities. Only by connecting with such and developing practices of resistance for the sake of a more just and humane reality can the existing system's idolatry be exposed.[5]

Rather than focusing only on what a few heroic individuals are going to do to overturn empire, which can feel like striking out naively at windmills, I propose that it is more appropriate and effective to nurture resistance from within faith communities. Thus, over the long-term they might become communities of resistance against the grain of empire's logic and script, wherever and however this is expressed. Resistance to empire happens where ambivalence is acknowledged, where the pressures of injustices are greatest, and when tensions are not prematurely resolved but addressed in concert with others. This begins to occur through a process of immanent critique that exposes the gap between the illusive promises and the actual realities in people's lives—through practices of seeing–remembering–connecting. By seeing, remembering, making connections *and* thus resisting for the sake of a more just and humane reality, the existing system's idolatry can be exposed.

5. This was developed more fully in my PhD dissertation, "Toward the Redemption," see especially 301, fn. 71.

Theology that has come out of imperial configurations has legitimated and furthered them, such as by depicting God or Christ in hierarchical, powerful, dominating, imperial ways. These reflect the dominant ways power operates under empire, in vivid contrast to the self-emptying power associated with Jesus, for example, in the second chapter of Philippians. Imperial configurations have also fuelled much missionary activity, and in subtle ways continue to influence how the church carries out its mission today, especially when driven at some level by a will to dominate, win over, or conquer others. Yet if Christ has overcome the powers of domination associated with empire, then the calling of the church is to proclaim and live this out in ways that transform and overcome rather than replicating patterns of domination that mark empire.

Theology is contextual and radically incarnate in and through people and throughout creation. Theology beckons us to go beyond the usual boundaries, distinctions, categories, and ways of organizing life. In that sense, it tends to be subversive. As transcontextual, it is ever cutting across new boundaries, challenging illusions, amnesia and injustices, and opening up transformative possibilities. Theology is what occurs when the Christian community knows itself to be living between text and context. It is that ongoing activity of the whole church that aims at clarifying what gospel must mean here and now. In this sense, as Douglas John Hall has pointed out, "gospel" is not a fixed, prescribed, once for all codification of truth. It becomes "good news." It is what has not yet been heard or known, not what is rote and predictable but surprising, bringing a new realization, introducing a new reality. It is news that is "good" because it challenges and displaces the "bad," offering another vision of what could be.

Moving beyond empire

The focus in much pastoral and theological discourse typically is on the individual, the freedom of the self, or on human subjectivity. However, this tends to reinforce the individualism that overlooks and enables the inter-structured realities of domination to hold sway. Under realities of domination, subjectivity is colonized at cultural, emotional, and spiritual levels. It becomes an expression or extension of empire. Admonishing people to be not so selfish or greedy is insufficient because it presupposes individualistic subjectivity. This individualistic focus, for example, is a shortcoming of many spiritual self-discovery movements, that broadly are a part of new age spirituality, and that tend to attract those who are of a higher, more secure class status.

It is because of how systemic domination permeates and pervades people's lives that we are impelled to consider the systemic, structural factors in which we and our world are enmeshed. Not exposing (seeing) and addressing this theologically is to neglect our calling. Pastoral care then focuses on adjusting to situations under which people are dominated/colonized/held captive, apart from the wider systemic factors in which society and the church are complicit. Focusing on individual sins is an unhelpful diversion, and leads to cynicism in relation to these larger reigning realities. The domination that keeps us from seeing needs to be exposed, along with the cycle in pursuit of "freedom" that perpetuates rather than challenging the domination.

In idolatry people seek salvation or liberation through political and religious submission to powers of domination. An idol becomes a veil of illusion, preventing us from seeing alternative ways of being or living.[6] "We become transformed into the idols we trust."[7] The invisible idol of commodities, money, marketing and capital becomes a pseudo-divine world that hovers over us, with its own laws that shape us. The promised utopia drains life from an ever-increasing number. The neoliberal promise is that economic growth and the sacrifices made will eventually benefit all or "trickle down."

Ironically, it is religion that usually is perceived as promulgating what is to be believed or accepted by faith, apart from empirical evidence. Economics has been presumed to be based on empirical data, and yet the clear evidence of the failure of neoliberalism in

6. Soelle, *Political Theology,* 111.

7. Ibid., 62–3.

the face of the 2008 economic crisis and its aftermath has apparently not been sufficient to sway the faith that policy makers still place in its basic tenets. The economy crashed when the purest form of this kind of economics was being pursued.

People are unable to recognize this when their "faith" continues to be lodged in the promise of succeeding in some sense, realizing some version of the promised American Dream: "you as in individual can make it if only you try hard enough." That promise continues to draw many to immigrate to the U.S., despite all the hurdles they face. People continue clinging to faith in the American Dream because most of the images and aspirations around them focus on those who have "made it/succeeded/gotten ahead." And thus, the blind desperate hope is that "I too might make it eventually." The desire of all grows in proportion to the growing wealth of only a few.

As I wrote in the 1980s with regard to white American working-class reality, "freedom" from domination is typically sought through the cycle of Individualism, Victimization, Privatization, which functions as a pseudo-trinity or idol, holding the reigning reality of domination in place.[8] Individualism puts the burden on the individual to succeed. Yet the pervasive experience of working people is that despite their works and hopes they have not acquired the fruits of this individualism. Consequently, there is a shift from individualism to a sense of victimization: "it was done to me." This in turn leads into a sense of passivity, resignation, or inevitability: "there's nothing that I as an individual can do about the forces out here." This results in "an intensified privatization of life, aided by an increasingly individualized, spiritualized a-historical theology, cut off from the systemic realities (such as racism and classism) that really do shape, dominate and violate people's lives. The illusion is perpetuated that the loss of being active subjects, under Victimization, results in regaining subjectivity through Privatization, but this is separated from and unable to transform what is holding people captive. Various political appeals today play into this. Here I am proposing that Seeing-Remembering-Connecting

8. Bloomquist, *The Dream Betrayed*, 52–53.

might become a counter to this trinity of Individualism, Victimization and Privatization that holds people in bondage.

Today many have become disillusioned with this dream of upward mobility, yet it still continues to be alluring. Its "eschatological" horizon is of the promised "good life." Yet this "effortocracy" in quest of "salvation," becomes an illusion that entraps, blinds us from seeing and acknowledging what is actually going on. Downward mobility is viewed as punishment for the "sin" of not trying hard enough. This becomes a closed self-perpetuating system holding people captive, as it shapes desire, values and actions in quest of the promised "salvation." In that sense it becomes a god-like idol in its rule over people's lives.

An increasing number of those who have "succeeded" in this system are beginning to acknowledge this, including those generally supportive of capitalism: "We live in a capitalist meritocracy that encourages individualism and utilitarianism, ambition and pride. But this society would fall apart if not for another economy, one in which gifts surpass expectations, in which insufficiency is acknowledged and dependence celebrated." [9]

For many ordinary Americans, the contradictions between what the dominant economic logic promises, and what it actually delivers has become much more evident, such as the lack of correlation between the stock market and the job market, and the huge gap between the very rich and the rest of the people. This feels like an increasingly betrayed promise to more and more—not only the poor and working class, but increasingly those who have been middle class. They increasingly are not seen (are overlooked) or remembered (are forgotten), and may feel like "losers," even in churches. They yearn for more than sympathy, for solidarity that can lead to transformation of the assumptions, systems and policies—the unquestioned system, or the gods to which they have been sacrificed.

When promises of the American Dream are betrayed, the underlying ideology can be exposed and transformed. However, this does not occur if we stand by passively without challenging its

9. Brooks, "The Structure of Gratitude," par. 12.

underlying tenets on theological grounds. An alternative, subversive subjectivity can begin to emerge, as resistance is formed over and against powers that would rob us of subjectivity. This might be expressed, for example, by resenting "higher ups" in the church, government or any institution telling folks what to do. Being a subject with agency to change this situation grows out of resisting the powers that rob us of subjectivity.

The Importance of Lament

The Old Testament book of Lamentations outlines the liturgical practice of social grief, contrasting what is actually the case with what was promised. "The imperial apparatus seems to thrive on a mix of self-confidence and anxiety that wants no embrace of loss."[10] Yet the truth is the durable force of historical loss; people know the reality of loss deeply and perennially. The truth of loss for Christians is found in the crucifixion, the ultimate disclosure of the power and love of God, which thus summons the faithful away from every seduction of empire.

Empires do not notice (see and remember) loss because they engage in a reality-denying ideology that covers over everything in the splendor of power, victory and stability. Empires are undeterred by inconvenient truths.[11] The Old Testament refrains of blessing David's kingship and Solomon's temple drown out the injustices in their midst. The certainty of God's blessings gave the people of Jerusalem an excuse to ignore or overlook the realities on the ground—especially the economic exploitation and political oppression going on—and which continues to occur today. The establishment is "well practiced in denial, because the liturgical mantra has covered over the failures of policies."[12] The poetry of truth-telling breaks the spell of the old ideologies, and begins to tell the truth about loss. Cries of lament, protest, indignation and

10. Brueggemann, *Out of Babylon*, 34–35.
11. Ibid., 36.
12. Ibid., 39.

insistence are transformed into practices of truth-telling for the sake of the bodily life of the world.

Thus, an especially urgent calling of churches and religious leaders is to point to the evidence and pose the critical questions—to open space for people to see-remember-connect. People are feeling acutely betrayed by the promises they have bought into, often with blind faith that now increasingly is feeling betrayed by powerful interests. These are determined to keep the market as "free" as possible, and through huge contributions, can hold politicians captive to their agendas.

Matters of basic meaning, hope and values are at stake, which should be the forte of the church. This false idolatry is exposed not primarily from top-down pronouncements, but from out of the actual contradictions as people have experienced them. The urgent pastoral task is to stand aside and open up ways for people to name and lament about the contradictions between what they have been promised, and what they are actually experiencing—inviting them to lament, and rage, even outrageously so.

People need to be able to grieve their loss and express their resentful sadness about what has been lost, raging for the world that is no more, lamenting for how standards of living and U.S. dominance in the world may be waning, for the sense of being abandoned, no longer blessed by a god who has been identified with success. Despair may be the defining pathology of our time, robbing the church of missional energy and stewardship generosity.[13] This is a despair that doubts God's fidelity to care and remember and doubts God's power to save. Thus, other means of "salvation" are pursued instead. As the economy declines, political temperatures can rise, often sparking anger and serious domestic unrest, attracted to what can be dangerous populist appeals.

Peter Laarman reflects on this new *kairotic* opportunity:

> I have a theory about what *might* begin to unfold if more religious leaders would step up to create sanctified spaces for real conversations about the New Normal. First, everything that is false and trumped up about our culture

13. Brueggemann, *Word Militant,* 139.

and our politics will stand fully exposed—including the lies and myths we tell ourselves about what it means to be "successful" and about the Pageant of Democracy put on by the plutocratic state.

Second, the people entering these sacred spaces will find themselves personally exposed in respect to what they really desire. . . . The godly desires thus exposed will turn out to be pretty basic ... companionship and a sense of shared enterprise . . . a whole lot more truth-telling in the public culture. They desire concrete ways of showing solidarity with others who likewise experience employer abuse and humiliation. They crave a chance to organize and to voice public outrage over the trashing of what little remains of the social contract in the United States.

Religion, in the sense of conventional piety, doesn't and shouldn't even enter into it. There's no real need for any kind of God talk in this context—and small group participants will be disturbed and offended if a sponsoring church tries to exploit their vulnerability for its own ulterior purposes. The meeting space will be sanctified not by anyone's particularist prayer but simply by the glory of God that is revealed when human beings come fully alive in an atmosphere that respects and welcomes them. I believe it's called *reverence*.[14]

Joerg Rieger puts the matter starkly: "only by declaring ourselves atheists in relation to the god of the market can we confess faith in the God become incarnate in Jesus Christ."[15] "The incarnation is a logic of downturn."[16] The incarnate One transcends a form of immanence determined by the status quo, in order to embrace a different form of immanence—on the margins. And that is likely to be subversive.

Resistance to empire is difficult since most people never fully realize what it is that shapes them. It reaches all the way into and creates their deepest desires. Desires are connected with their

---

14. Laarman, "Humiliation and 'Success.'" par. 10–13.

15. Rieger, *No Rising Tide*, 133.

16. Ibid., 130.

transcendental promise.[17] This calls for resisting desire as it has been constructed and being open to the emergence of alternative desires that have to do with my good in relation to the good of others. This erupts not from above, but from below, from the underside, as we look outward and pursue solidarity with those who truly are left out, around us and around the world. There "God labors in solidarity with the people and resisting desire spreads from there."[18]

17. Miguez, et al., *Beyond the Spirit of Empire*, 39.

18. Ibid., 16.

5

Why *Seeing–Remembering–Connecting*?

In late 2011, the multifaceted Occupy Wall Street movement emerged, and spread to hundreds of sites around the US and throughout the world. The "1 percent versus 99 percent" slogan caught on with more and more people because, in its bluntness, it spoke to the distress that they were experiencing; it articulated and focused their outrage, and continues to do so today (when nearly 99 percent of new wealth is going to the top 1 percent). Although institutional churches were not necessarily leading or directing what was occurring in 2011, faith-grounded leaders were visibly present, along with many others.

Overtly, the Occupy movement was secular, but interlaced with rituals, symbols, and practices that resonated with religious traditions and practices. These included

- *Lamenting*: People were giving voice and expression to the outrage that people feel, rather than wallowing in despair.

- *Naming and speaking truth to power*: The movement has focused on naming and speaking out to corporate and financial powers, not unlike that of the targeted attacks by Old Testament prophets and prophetic church spokespersons in the past.

- *Envisioning*: The young were raising up visions, encapsulated in slogans that drew diverse people together people, and insisting that change indeed is possible.

- *Connecting*: Diverse people were connecting (through social networking and "human mics"), communicating across boundaries that usually separate them, and obviously enjoying being together.

- *Local-global linkages:* links were quickly developed with movements also occurring then in Egypt and in Wisconsin, between global and local injustices, between economic, climate and an array of other justice movements.

- *Caring for one another:* care, compassion and respect for one another was nurtured in practical ways, such as providing food and medical care.

- *Symbols that speak deeply and move people*: The creative signs and symbols drew people together and stirred them (such as a Golden Calf being carried down Wall Street), as religious symbols have long functioned.

- *Rituals*: Drumming, singing, dancing, chanting and moving together empowered and inspired participants with visions and a resilient, transcendent hope that another world is possible, as occurs through lively liturgical worship.

- *Staying power for the long-haul:* The encampments of the Occupy movement did not go away overnight, a faint reminder of how the church's ongoing commitment to work for God's justice in the world is a long struggle that continues throughout history.[1]

This was when it dawned on me of the need to connect what was occurring with verbs that also connect with practices that are at the heart of faith communities. Eventually this came into focus for me in the triad of "seeing–remembering–connecting." Although the broad Occupy movement may have faded since then, or evolved into renewed advocacy on more focused issues, overall this could have become a kind of collective wake-up call to churches and other faith traditions—of what they need to be

1. These practices first were listed in Bloomquist, "*Ekklesia*," 62–63.

saying and doing amid the ongoing economic, political and environmental crises.

Probably what they especially hold in common is that, at their core, both the Occupy movement and the church have to do with practices that together are subversive of unjust realities. As Walter Brueggemann maintains, the church is the last place around where a sub-version of reality can be articulated and an alternative vision held forth.[2]

> The Old Testament is essentially de-privileged testimony that construes the world alternatively . . . evidence offered by a community of those who at first were nomads or peasants and later exiles . . . thus, far from the hegemonic seats of power and centers of certitude . . . telling a tale of reality that [confounds] the consensus put together by those with power.[3]

What I am proposing here is that practices of seeing−remembering−connecting are a way of picking up on the energy ignited through the Occupy movement, doing so with language and practices more immediately and universally recognizable. Seeing−remembering−connecting is what biblical sources, traditions, and the movements they inspire have long been about. Yet they are common verbs to which people unaccustomed to theological jargon can readily relate. They can be grasped in quite secular ways, but also bear theological significance. For Luther and others, the finite bears what is infinite. They are everyday practices that also become habits that continually are repeated.

Not only do perspectives and dynamics influenced and shaped through faith traditions have practical relevance, but they also can become subversive of the systemic injustices in which we are immersed. How can this occur or become more evident? Because most people are so immersed in the systemic injustices referred to in the previous chapter as "empire," they often are not (or don't want to be) aware of the injustices, or they feel powerless to do much about such. For only a few have the injustices become

2. Brueggemann, *Word Militant*, 18.

3. Ibid., 125.

so blatant and motivating that they readily respond to appeals to take on and challenge such, sometimes in risky ways. This might involve polarizing rhetoric or tactics that others shy away from, especially because of the benefits *they* still hope to gain from "the way things are." Appearing to be subversive of what currently is dominating our common life is not popular in most established congregations (see chapter 2).

Thus, what becomes key is the twofold strategy that Martin Luther used in taking on both the subjective and objective aspects of the systemic domination in his day. The domination system needs to be unveiled in terms of what people themselves are experiencing—the "seeing" must break through the social blindness—rather than people being told from the outside, or by various media or authorities who tell them what they are to see. Yet, a critical interpretative dimension is brought to this by remembering the substance of faith traditions, as well as experiences of family and communities that are contrary to what the official scripts in society proclaim. This is potentially subversive of what currently is occurring. When leaders do not give adequate attention to this remembering dimension *and draw out its critical potential*, then lapsing into nostalgic "good old days" and political appeals that try to "go back" are all too tempting, and dangerous. This must and can be resisted when leaders make connections between what people are experiencing and remembering *and* the interlinked systemic injustices. This potentially leads to solidarity across boundaries of "us versus them" that have justified unjust social orders, and which need to be de-stabilized.

An incident in the congregation I was pastoring in the early 1980s in Brooklyn, New York illustrates this. During a Wednesday evening Lenten series, I asked the parishioners to read a brief article on the oppression that was occurring then in Central America. This unleashed their seeing and expressing out loud (some for the first time) their own experiences of oppression and abuse as white working-class workers. This was followed almost immediately by their connecting their experience with what was happening to church folk in Central America, and the role of the

U.S. government in perpetuating abuses there. Not only that evening did they begin advocating for what U.S. policies needed to change, but when I returned to visit the congregation the next year, a member I had perceived as conservative and apolitical proudly announced to me that the city-wide commemoration of the assassination of Archbishop Romero would occur that year in this small congregation, a congregation that previously had been uninvolved in such matters. The remembering and connecting that came alive that evening has inspired me ever since.

What is pure gift (God's grace) needs to be reflected in a community's practices. In addition to the customary church practices, this means being with and for those who suffer. The eucharistic union between a believer and Christ nurtures union between the believer and neighbors. Through the indwelling Christ, we are made one with others.[4]

When intentionally practiced by a community over time, these practices *together* become a subversive declaration of who and whose we are in the midst of those forces that dominate, oppress and shape us according to their power and interests, and that usually immobilize us from being activated to change injustices. This becomes more apparent through the consciousness-raising practices implicit in seeing–remembering–connecting. To begin naming what we are up against signals that confessing faith in this kind of God clearly can be dangerous or at least risky; they provoke reactions. Yet "[t]he one narrated and revealed between Good Friday and Pentecost as God's own Son constitutes the revolutionary *subversion* [emphasis mine] of all human thought and expectation, embodying the utter contrast between God's kingdom and ours."[5]

The church as the body of Christ is called to embody and live this out, in witness to the incarnation. The incarnation is itself God's supreme occupation. This is a conviction of faith that must be enacted and lived out—through practices—if it is to be credible to secular skeptics doubtful that religious traditions are still relevant today. Together we are empowered to cooperate and

4. Moe-Lobeda, *Healing a Broken World,* 89.
5. Lewis, 310.

organize with others to resist these powers reigning over our lives and world.

This triad of verbs corresponds to three of the major pathologies pervading North American society today, as well as much of the rest of world: illusion, amnesia, and individualism (separateness).

Illusions:

> A public that can no longer distinguish between truth and fiction is left to interpret reality through illusion. The worse reality becomes, the more people seek refuge and comfort in illusions . . . lies and distortions become truth and people can believe what they want to believe. *Blind faith in illusions is our culture's secular version of being born again* [emphasis mine]. . . . The culture of illusion, one of happy thoughts, manipulated emotions, and trust in the beneficence of those in power, means we sing along with the chorus or are instantly disappeared from view like the losers on a reality show.[6]

Although much of this illusion is generated by advertising and other corporate powers that benefit from our deception, this has also taken over the political scene today, causing more and more to feel cynical and drop out. Rather than trusting what we can actually see for ourselves—seeing is believing—we are submerged instead in illusions that create our world. Such illusions numb us and deter the emergence of democratic participation in our common life.

Social amnesia:

> Historical consciousness and truth are now sacrificed to the spectacles of consumerism, celebrity culture, hyped-up violence and a market-driven obsession with the self. . . . Public values and the public good have now been reduced to nostalgic reminders of another era. . . . Market-driven values get normalized by erasing any viable

6. Hedges, *Empire of Illusion*, 10–15.

understanding of history, memory, power, ideology and politics. . . . Without the necessary formative culture that can provide Americans with a language that enables them to recognize the political, economic and social causes of their problems, a politics of despair, anger and dissatisfaction can easily be channeled into a politics of violence, vengeance and corruption, feeding far right-wing movements willing to trade in bigotry, thuggery and brutality.[7]

Journalists in parts of the world suffering continual calamities allege that political leaders suffer from social amnesia: "Because most of our politicians ignore the tools of memory which would make them relevant to our present world, they address critical political and social issues from entirely insensate feelings."[8]

Individualism is the master narrative that those in power, the dominant subjects, those who have succeeded, tell about themselves. It becomes the lens through which we see and interpret what is going on in our lives and that of others. Individualism functions to covers up and repress the real, that is, all who have contributed to their success and on whose backs their success has been built.[9] Whatever has been repressed becomes the truth of the system, which needs to be exposed. "Others" are feared because they have the power to unravel the subjectivity of those in power. In this sense, individualism helps to support empire. It leads to a separation of issues and of persons who are different from "us."

The framework of seeing–remembering–connecting is more immediately accessible to those for whom theological jargon may seem alien or outdated. Seeing-remembering-connected is basic to what it means to be human, and thus a way that can open up some deeply theological insights that are critical, historical and relational.

These verbs (through translation) are also more universally accessible across cultures, including globally. They are

7. Giroux, "Living in the Age of Imposed Amnesia," par. 2–9.

8. Magoda, "Uganda: Our Leaders Suffer from Social Amnesia," par. 1.

9. Miguez, et al., *Beyond the Spirit of Empire, 48.*

trans-cultural. "Outsiders" or newcomers are often able to see what most of us who long have been living in North America cannot see. Others can remember across much longer spans of history (and prehistory) than we can, and with intrinsic interconnections or relationships with all human beings and creation. The Ubunta saying, "I am because we are" encapsulates this. Perspectives from other cultures as to how we come to know and act, help to wake us up when we are clouded over with illusions, forgetfulness, and separateness.

We implore others to help us to see, remember, and connect what we would not otherwise. Seeing–remembering–connecting leads to a kind of turning about or conversion, from the separateness of individuals or issues, toward new ways of being and connecting with others, including those most different from us. Through this framework, new deeper kinds of solidarity can come alive—in our communities as well as across the world—not as an end in themselves, but for the transformation of systemic injustices.

Seeing–remembering–connecting is a distinctly visual turn, which is important today. We have entered the age of "visualcy," the third great transformation in the way that human beings engage and interpret their world. The first was orality, when what was most significant was communicated and passed on from one generation to another in the form of oral traditions (especially stories). The Christian movement originated in the long period of transition from orality (Jesus spoke to a largely oral culture) to the age of literacy (shaped by the written Bible). But now the most compelling and significant information is communicated visually. To be sure, just as literate people do not cease to speak, visually oriented people do not cease to read. However, as a culture shifts from literacy to visualcy, greater weight must be given to communicating through what can been *seen* rather than only through what is heard.

This is a shift away from what often is associated with passivity—a posture of receiving grace from God rather than anything we do—to our being empowered from what is outside ourselves.

Grace or the indwelling Christ in us in what empowers us to see, remember, connect. In a sense, seeing is more than hearing. It is an active cognition; because of what we see (what is wrong or unjust) we are activated to act. When we continue to go along with illusions, of what appears to be but is not really the case, *then* we passively submit to the injustices. Then life "freezes over;" then we are dominated by sin. We overlook or forget and become ever more disconnected from others, and from the life God intends for us. Given the powers that do dominate our lives and the realities under which we live, such a stance eventually becomes subversive of such, through ongoing practices. If the kinds of domination and empire outlined previously are to be subverted or transformed, what is needed is a seeing–remembering–connecting that goes against the grain of what currently prevails.

This focus is akin to the "Christian practices" turn in theology in recent decades, with books and articles too numerous to list here. The emphasis is not on theology as an abstract discipline, but theology that makes practical differences in society. Specifically here the emphasis is on faith-based *praxis* that becomes transformative of the domination. Practical theology is theological reflection that is grounded in the life of the church, society, and the individual. It both critically recovers the theology of the past and constructively develops theology for the future.

As discussed previously, empire progressively incorporates the entire world within its open, expanding borders. This dynamic creates the very world it inhabits (Hardt and Negri) through the sacrifices it demands. Those who are thus sacrificed tend to be deleted from the memory of those who succeed. Instead, their sufferings are interpreted as necessary on the path to the hoped for "salvation" that the powers of domination promise. The meta-narrative of "transcendent illusions" that is generated by empire provides a criterion for interpreting reality; it imposes a never reached horizon.[10] To counter this kind of "transcendence," a framework is required in which this sacrificial logic does not

10. Ibid., 89.

prevail, but through which instead we are empowered to work for a more human and just social and ecological order.

Seeing–remembering–connecting is one such possible framework. This is a kind of seeing that evokes remembering, that gives depth or perspective and thus propels us to connect and act across boundaries. The three together embody a sense of transcendence—going beyond the surface givens, into what might be. We are impelled by an eschatological sense that another world is possible.

This is what a prophetic pastoral ministry is about: uncovering what is really going on and connecting across boundaries. It is what the dominant prevailing order doesn't want us to see, remember, and connect. It is what the tradition of critical theory was getting at. It involves moving from a sense of powerlessness to that of empowered action in community. Seeing–remembering–connecting are practices nurtured and carried out again and again, because new faces of systemic injustices are continually appearing. It is an ongoing *praxis* of what it means to be church, in collaboration *with* rather than set over and against those with different faith perspectives.

I personally experienced "seeing–remembering–connecting" in the following:

For some years, a large conglomerate has been planning to build a huge coal terminal in the northwest corner of Washington State (projected to transport 50 million tons of coal each year to Asia). The early assumption was that the Lummi Nation and others would favor the promised jobs and economic development this would bring.

In September 2012, leaders of the Lummi Nation invited the public, to "come and *see* Cherry Point (*Xwe'chi'eXen*)." This is a rocky undeveloped shoreline and deep water bay of the Salish Sea (north Puget Sound) that has been their fishing grounds, on a beautiful land overlooking Bellingham Bay, sacred land of the Lummis for thousands of year. A sign connected Jerusalem, Gettysburg, and Cherry Point—identifying them all as "sacred sites."

Here on the shoreline, the Lummis were *remembering* the stories of suffering, both before and after contact with European settlers. They remember their countless ancestors whose bones from many generations are still buried in this land or at the bottom of the sea. These are sacred memories that sustain their identity and sense of being a people today. They remember when fish were more plentiful in these waters, before oil tankers began transiting these waters, catching up fish traps in their wake. And, they remember the Great Spirit who opposes this. Emboldened by this remembering, they make public their refusal to be bought off, which is vividly symbolized in the burning of a huge facsimile of a multi-million dollar check marked "non-negotiable."

Further, the Lummi people *connect* the exploitation of the land and water that has long been a part of their narrative, with the profit-driven corporate interests who now want to build a coal terminal here, occupying and destroying land and water further. They connect what is proposed here, not only with the exploitation they have long experienced, but also with what this will do to the air globally. If this area were to become complicit in the shipping of such massive amounts of coal, when burned, this would contribute significantly to climate change. The whole of the earth, water, air, in their fragile inter-related web would be further destroyed. Further, they *connect* with non-Native people who share these waters (e.g., with non-native commercial fishers), and who join them in organized resistance to this development. This resistance movement has continued to grow and expand.

What has become increasingly evident is how the spirituality, values and resistance of the Lummi Nation, when connected with many other tribal governments in the Northwest, as well as with a host of environmental organizations and faith-based communities, are now at the energizing heart of the years of resistance to this controversial project. Most prominently, for each year (starting in 2013) a massive totem pole has been carved and ceremoniously transported thousands of miles to many tribal lands in states and provinces across the Northwest, reaching millions of people, and connecting with many other sites where fossil fuels are being extracted and transported.

In 2015, Pope Francis' *Laudato Si* gave new impetus for connecting with faith communities in what is now themed, "Sharing Responsibility for Creation and each other."

6

Subversive Seeing

Seeing in the New Testament

That which was from the beginning, which we have
heard, which we have seen with our eyes, which we have
looked upon and touched with our hands concerning
the word of life—the life was made manifest and we saw
it, and testify to it, and proclaim to you the eternal life
which was with the Father and was made manifest to
us—that which we have seen and heard we proclaim also
to you . . . (1 John 1:1–3; ESV).

Jesus said, "Receive your sight; your faith has saved you." (Luke
18:42) Seeing is closely connected with believing; as the common
adage originally attributed in John's Gospel to Thomas puts it,
"seeing is believing." In John, *not* seeing is considered sin.[1]

To "see God" in Jesus' act of healing is to recognize the truth
of the Word becoming flesh,[2] a dynamic truth that challenges assumptions, systems and structures of privilege. The story is permeated with theological meanings. Throughout most of the story
in the ninth chapter of John, Jesus himself is silent; most of the
narrative is focused instead on a human dialogue about seeing and
believing. There were various cultural stigma or barriers attached
to those who were marginalized because they were unable to see.

1. O'Day, "John," 574.
2. Ibid., 575.

After regaining sight, the man says: "though I was blind, now I see"(John 9:25). Jesus says, "I came . . . so that those who do not see may see, and those who do see may become blind"(John 9:39). The blind one sees clearly what God is about, while those who believe they can see are those who are truly blind. Jesus subverts what can be seen; he shifts the interpretive framework.

Too often John's Gospel has been misread as a religious text that is removed from, not participating in societal, political, economic and cultural realities.[3] In spiritualized, individualistic interpretations, incarnate bodies living in economic and political structures don't matter much. But in the world of John's Gospel, religion is public, societal, communal, and quite political.[4] "Believing" and having "eternal life" are shaped by the actions of transformation and socio-political conflict occurring throughout the Gospel. Those to whom this Gospel is addressed were not a sect separated from society, but participants who were acculturated in society, regularly negotiating over what it means to live *in* but not be *of* the empire, sometimes accommodating, other times resisting.

Concludes Warren Carter: "John's Gospel is a 'hidden transcript,' part of a debate among Jesus-believers over imperial negotiation, yet contesting imperial power. The rhetoric tries to create lines between the empire and faithful followers of Jesus, urging Jesus-believers to a less-accommodated and more distinctive way of life as an alternative community."[5] In this light, "resurrection means restoration and transformation, not just of individuals but also of God's world and human communities. It signifies the end of imperial power and damage and the establishment of God's life-giving and just purposes."[6]

Christ's special connection to the underside of empire is manifest throughout his earthly ministry, as recorded throughout the Gospels, and especially through his being crucified by the Roman Empire. Yet if Christ has overcome the powers of domination

3. Carter, *John and Empire*, 4.
4. Ibid., 7.
5. Ibid., 82.
6. Ibid., 329.

associated with empire, he did so far more subtly and effectively than through force or dominating conquest. He did so especially through the many incidents, parables and dialogues recorded in the Gospels where he invited, challenged, even provoked people to *see* differently from how they were conditioned to through the reigning religious, social and political categories and powers of that day.

Jesus heals those blind; he peels away what clouds vision. This suggests a pivotal meaning of "seeing" for our purposes here: clearing away what clouds, obfuscates or hinders us from seeing what really is. "[W]hen we nurture blindness, contort our vision and memories, stifle our imagination and hope, and ignore portions of who we are . . . we acquiesce, rather than resist."[7]

Seeing subversively today

The focus here is on a multi-faceted seeing enables a kind of transcendence to break through the structures and ideological mandates reigning over ordinary people's lives. Through remembering, new visions or perspectives on social realities begin to emerge. This in turn necessitates and empowers change in the structured injustices in which people and the rest of creation are enmeshed. Seeing breaks in from beyond, both spatially and historically, and shifts our horizons. What we can see, moves us beyond closed systems that encapsulate us and usually are taken for granted.

- Today in the US, the increasing practice of police wearing body cameras has given ordinary citizens a new lens into seeing what occurs when someone is apprehended. This has begun to alter public views of police use of force and race relations.

- A man recalled that when he was five years old he went along with his father (a pastor) to visit a farm worker family in rural Washington. As a child he was shocked to see the meager conditions in which the migrant families were living

7. Moe-Lobeda, *Healing a Broken World*, 68.

in the horse stalls of a barn. The next school year the teacher insisted that Abraham Lincoln had put on end to slavery in the U.S. The young boy countered the teacher, protesting that slavery has not ended, but was still occurring in his community. His teacher refused to believe him, countering what he had actually seen with the official textbook version.

- "Seeing" was revelatory in a 2008 LWF climate change event in India in which I participated. We stood on the shore and looked out to the sea of the Bay of Bengal. Beside us on the beach were the shells of large turtles whose habitat had been destroyed. A few hundred yards out to sea was a sandbar shining golden in the sun, which would be submerged in another two months. Only a few years ago that shining sandbar was a lively fishing village. Now there is nothing—no houses, no animals, no trees. The village had been swallowed by the sea. Like several other villages along the coast, the sea had inundated the coastline and swallowed all before it. Fifteen years ago, said one fisherman, the shoreline was five kilometers away. Now it was only a few hundred meters away. Nearby, trees have been planted to help hold back the further encroachment of the sea into the land, as well as protecting the Hindu temple that has replaced the previous temple that disappeared into the sea.

The practice of "seeing" has more theological significance than has usually been assumed, especially in Protestant traditions that have focused *not* on seeing (on what is visual), but on hearing the orally proclaimed Word. However, in order to treat the Word of God with the awe it deserves, we must take into account the practices of seeing. God is not seen but is testified to in a particular way of seeing. The more we see, the more we hear. To hear the word aright requires a certain amount of seeing.

Seeing implies what can be glimpsed through the senses, rather than what is mostly theoretical and abstract. Seeing is empirical, and incarnate. The common, the ordinary, what is experienced or sensed gains theological interest or significance. God is known in the ordinary—in what is familiar, close at hand, quotidian. Yet seeing also is perceiving, an understanding on many levels. Contrary to popular views, seeing is *not* what individuals can do on their own. We see as part of and in relation to community; the assumptions, values and worldviews of such affect us and what we focus on or ignore. Seeing has to do with what comes from outside of ourselves. Others provoke us to see what we would not on our own, as well as provoking us to see ourselves differently.

"What we see, and refuse to see and how we see are morally loaded, bearing upon whether we foster or thwart liberative change. False sight cripples moral agency."[8] Critical and morally responsible sight in necessary. "'Critical seeing' burns people up, unless it is also wedded to seeing, in the same gaze, a second reality . . . the life-giving, life-saving, life-sustaining power of God coursing through the *communio* and through all creation, a God whose love for this world cannot be thwarted by any force on heaven or earth."[9]

Seeing also is akin to what sometimes is understand as mysticism. It is seeing God in all things and all things in God, in a way that Sallie McFague insists is radically incarnational. We see God in the face of Jesus: "For it is the God who said 'let light shine in the darkness' who has shone in our hearts to give the light of the knowledge of God in the face of Jesus Christ"(2 Cor. 4:6). We develop a "double vision:" seeing at the same time everything as it is *and* everything in God.[10] Rather than envisioning God as a being, God is that from which all else derives its reality, and thus frees us from being captive to illusions.

Dorothee Soelle points out that mysticism is part of the endeavor to escape from the fate of language that seeks to control, possess and dominate.[11] Democratizing mysticism means discerning it in the everyday forms of nonconformist life. Mysticism lifts

8. Ibid., 9.

9. Moe-Lobeda, "Communio and a Spirituality of Resistance," 153.

10. McFague, *New Climate for Theology,* 164.

11. Soelle, *Silent Cry*, 63.

experiences out of the abstractness of religious doctrine.[12] Being united with God, we see the world with God's eyes. We see what otherwise is rendered invisible, irrelevant or trivial, in a mysticism of "wide open eyes." [13] This is not necessarily a new relationship with God but a different relationship to the world—one that borrows the "eyes" of God. According to Soelle, mysticism makes resistance and liberation possible. When we only stare at the lords of this world and the mass of individuals rendered harmless, we do yet have new eyes for seeing. Instead, "Mysticism and transformation are indissolubly interconnected. Without economic and ecological justice and without God's preferential love for the poor and for this planet, the love for God and the longing for oneness seems to be to be an atomistic illusion."[14]

From Illusions toward Truth-telling

Today, much of seeing is socially conditioned to become a distraction or diversion from what really matters; it is seeing that entertains rather than leading toward greater understanding. Thus, attention must be given to seeing that exposes "the big picture" of what is actually occurring, rather than what is assumed in customary or officially authorized interpretations, or reigning myths and ideologies that portend to be true or authoritative. This calls for seeing through the pretenses, honestly and authentically, seeing beneath the surface of what is assumed to be the case. Helping people to see, especially in delving deeper into what is going on is an intrinsically spiritual, pastoral, *and* prophetic practice. Thus, we are proposing here that it is a crucial faith practice. How might this be pursued in ways that lead toward the transformation rather than legitimation of the spirit, logic and practices of domination that hold people captive and generate injustices in our day?

12. Ibid., 18.
13. Ibid., 283.
14. Ibid., 89.

Resistance to such may be difficult to inculcate in U.S. churches, but the starting point is to interpret Scripture with a social hermeneutic that can open people's eyes to see what comes to us day after day in current events. The biblical texts, in which social analysis often is implicit, engage us in contesting between dominant power and truth-telling. People need to be invited to hear these texts intentionally, so that accommodation or resistance can be considered knowingly, with an openness that lives in the hope for new possibilities.[15] Living in a situation of exile, Hebrew Jews did not abandon faith or wallow is despair or retreat to privatized religion. Instead, this resulted in daring theological articulations, news about a dynamic God that cannot be suppressed.

Instead of blind faith, filled with whatever has popular appeal at the time, what begins to emerge is a substantial gutsy well-tested faith, a subversive seeing that takes seriously the datum of what is occurring today. This sees patterns, brings to light systemic injustice and the seductive dynamics of empire, and reinterprets biblical/theological traditions in relation to such. This is a resilient confessing faith, not one that is complicit in what is occurring, but that can boldly challenge the assumptions, practices, and outcomes, in light of the alternative utopic vision of the reign of God—the good news that another world is possible. We can see because, as those baptized into a new reality, our eyes are opened and we are "en-couraged" to see or discern what we would not otherwise. We are provoked to *see*, not as spectators but as those pulled into the action, into the drama, into the story then and the story unfolding now.

> Jesus did not live in order to die; rather, he died in order to live—in order that all of us might see a new way to live. ... We do not see the face of God directly, but we meet God in the face of Jesus, in Jesus eating with outcast, healing the sick, destabilizing the wealthy and powerful, welcoming the stranger, siding with the oppressed, and inviting everyone to the table. *This* is the glory of God

15. Brueggemann, *Out of Babylon,* 152–53.

that we see in the face of Jesus: we see that a different world is possible.[16]

And that is bound to be subversive.

The theologically-empowered "seeing" that I am proposing is the kind of seeing that exposes and critiques systems of domination, as discussed in chapter 4. The Western tradition of critique was originally synonymous with "reason" as an endless questioning in search of truth. This kind of reason was rooted in social conditions, such that critique of such became an impetus for transformative *praxis*. But in the modern era, reason became more subjective and increasingly instrumentalized to serve any end. It became dependent on self-interest, habit or conformity, and subject to ideological manipulation. Such subjective reason goes along with rather than critiquing domination. Domination acquires its own "rationality."

Survival depends on adapting to systemic domination that feels overpowering: "you gotta go along with it." Economic and social forces become blind "natural" forces that we attempt to control by adjusting to them, by turning increasingly to the private arena, there to seek fulfillment under the illusion that this is space "free" from domination. The domination functions as an absolute, an idol to which sacrifices are made. These insights from critical theory (drawing from Horkheimer, Adorno, Aronowitz, etc.) help uncover how domination occurs not only through economic activity but also how it is perpetuated through family, education, mass culture, leisure life, *and* through religion.

Instead, an immanent critique of life begins to emerge as people confront the promise with the reality. What is theoretically promised is critiqued on the basis of what we are actually experiencing and seeing in our lives and communities. This is a radically immanent exposing of how domination has been mystified, through a kind of "transcendence as radical immanence."[17] We cannot just attack the reigning ideology without engaging and thus

16. McFague, *New Climate for Theology*, 39.

17. Driver, *Patterns of Grace*, 164.

transforming the subjective and objective aspects of such domination. An alternative subversive subjectivity begins to emerge.
Being a subject with agency grows out of resistance against the
powers that rob us of subjectivity. This may be expressed through
resentment against "higher-ups" in any institution—including the
church—telling us what to do.

Suddenly, how empire dominates reality no longer seem so
absolute or without ambivalence. Resistance to such involves a re-
versal: those who assumed they were secure in their subjectivities
lose it, and those most vulnerable find it (similar to the contrast in
Matt 16:25). An alternative subjectivity exposes the false subjectivity operating under domination.

But to resist over the long haul, we need to form habits that
come from remembering and inhabiting certain traditions. Seeing
by itself is not sufficient.

7

Subversive Remembering

"Do you have eyes and fail to see? Do you have ears and fail to hear? And do you not *remember*?" (Mark 8:18) "Do you not *remember* the five loaves for the five thousand, and how many baskets you gathered?" (Matt 16:9) Repeatedly throughout the New Testament, the disciples are depicted as forgetting and then remembering what Jesus had said, in ways that they didn't quite get before.

What kind of remembering?

As commonly understood, to "remember" is to bring to mind or think of again. In remembering we interpret what we see or discern in relationship to whom or whose we are, and who or what has been forgotten or overlooked across time and space. Remembering is a present activity that draws from the past for the sake of the future, in contrast to a nostalgia that tends to idealize and get stuck in the past. The focus here is on remembering that leads to questioning, to critique of what is generally accepted, and to empowering transformation of what is. In other words, remembering has political implications for the present and the future. Remembering also becomes a deeply theological matter, a dynamic process that makes present again, and leans into the future.

A key aspect of the challenge to be addressed here is *systemic amnesia* across time and space—silencing, covering over, refusing to see what is truthful or not—especially the wider systemic political, economic, cultural matters that influence and shape our lives. "America has become amnesiac—a country in which forms of historical, political, and moral forgetting are not only willfully practiced but celebrated."[1]

Remembering counters systemic amnesia. Remembering is counter-cultural, especially in regions of this society where social memory (history) is short or nonexistent. For instance, the Pacific Northwest region of North America (also known as "Cascadia") has long lacked a dominant overarching narrative, such that the individual becomes the center of all experience. Here, in this most utopic of regions, an environmental spiritualism tends to prevail over affiliation with religious (or other) institutions. Area artists, reflecting on their implicitly spiritual creations in response to the effects of climate change, adamantly insist that their works are not "religious"[2] because they do want to be associated with any religious tradition. Except among indigenous peoples (see example at end of chapter 5), there usually is little focus on collective memories. As Patricia O'Connell Killian provocatively asks, "Can and does this place, in which so many experience themselves to be free from the past, from tradition, and from constraining ties, inspire a vision compelling enough to viably reweave the bonds of humans with each other and with the "more-than-human" world for a twenty-first century, global people?"[3]

In dramatic contrast in some parts of the world, remembering goes back millennia. For example, in the midst of the 2015 Greek debt crisis, critical connections were made with developments 2600 years ago in Greece that led to direct democracy and being freed from bondage to debt, and which empowers their struggles today. At the center of nearly every community in Europe, monuments have been erected that remember what has occurred there, going back hundreds of years. Whereas in the U.S. old buildings typically have been torn down, in most parts of Europe, they tend

1. Giroux, "The Violence of Organized Forgetting," par. 1.

2. As I heard at the "Nature in Balance" exhibit at the Whatcom Museum, August 1, 2013.

3. Killian, "Memory, Novelty and Possibility," 67.

to be preserved as new roads and developments are built around them.

When memory is eroded, people are deprived of how remembered tradition can resource them today. A community's memory provides accumulated insights into how things came about, into what we human beings are up against. The danger is that in becoming a memory-less, tradition-less society, we become incapable of empathetic responses to the claims of other living beings, much less of the rest of creation.

Remembering becomes crucial, for example, in the midst of the extensive waves of the migration of people occurring in our time. It is tempting to forget the massive previous efforts (such as during the 1940s) to receive and provide for refugees from war, hunger and persecution. Remember instead: "You shall love the alien as yourself, for you were aliens in the land of Egypt."(Lev 19:34b) In many communities today, remembering what has occurred previously is motivating and empowering collective responses.

The way many Protestants in the U.S. have learned to "do church" has militated against a strong and nurturing connection to the past.[4] Instead, the American mantra is to let go and move on. Churches with less historical baggage or ties to one tradition are considered by some to be more "successful." Many people consider history an obstacle to toleration[5] because of how it has supported intolerance in the past.

This lack of historical memory is in contrast to congregations like the one I served in a rural area in Washington state. Unlike most in this region, this congregation was surrounded by a cemetery. Buried there are many ancestors of this historically old congregation that has in recent years questioned whether it will survive. But one of the patriarchs insists that he will not let this church die, because his ancestors are buried all around it. Newcomers are drawn to the wall covered with confirmation class

4. Bendroth, *Spiritual Practice of Remembering*, 80.
5. Ibid., 87.

photos, and to heritage festivals for the newcomers in the community who have little sense of its history.

This easily can lapse into a nostalgia that only seeks to conserve the past. But such remembering can also have subversive potential, nurturing practices that welcome newcomers, that defy some of the prevailing ideologies, and that are life-giving for creating a future not bound to what big churches or denominational authorities tell them to be or do to be "successful." In resistance to this, through remembered narratives people find the strength to keep going amid ever-new challenges.

> Without the necessary formative culture that can provide Americans with a language that enables them to recognize the political, economic and social causes of their problems, a politics of despair, anger and dissatisfaction can easily be channeled into a politics of violence, vengeance and corruption, feeding far right-wing movements willing to trade in bigotry, thuggery and brutality.[6]

Remembering how historical developments came about can peel away illusions and illuminate what we are facing today. For example, the huge upsurge in corporate control over political processes did not just happen. What needs to be remembered is a key secret strategy memo that Lewis Powell wrote in 1971 for the U.S. Chamber of Commerce.[7] The memo became a rallying cry among corporate executives for how to reassert corporate dominance over the American economy and its government, which it had lost during the era of the New Deal. The memo openly stated that corporations should punish their political enemies, seek political power through both the law and politics, and use political power aggressively.

This corporate domination over economic, political and legal domains has increased ever since, with most people unaware of this scenario that was ignited nearly half a century ago. Many still continue to *believe,* contrary to what they see and experience, that a growing economy raises wages and family incomes across

6. Giroux, "Living in the Age of Imposed Amnesia," par. 9.

7. Powell, "Attack on the Free Enterprise System," 158, 160.

the board. The economy did work somewhat like this during the "golden age," from the end of World II until the early 1970s, when prosperity was widely shared and income inequality declined. But since then we increasingly have experienced a "gilded age of inequality." The rich have gotten fabulously richer, while the middle class has struggled and more workers have fallen into poverty. Now huge contributions of only a few billionaires are holding candidates and democratic election processes hostage. Increasingly the U.S. is becoming a plutocracy rather than a democracy. As former President Jimmy Carter puts it, "we've just seen a complete subversion of our political system."[8]

It is crucial to remember what has been forgotten or overlooked in our officially optimistic, classist society, where the "losers" disappear and drop from memory in families, communities, and society as a whole. Only those who succeed are remembered. They are the self-made individuals who appear to succeed apart from or even despite their community and history.

Instead, remembering the losers and their history opens up a wider critical social analysis. It also opens up greater possibilities for solidarity with those "left behind" in much of the rest of the world. It irrupts from below. It is remembering what the interests of domination or empire would prefer be overlooked. It leads toward questioning or critiquing what is for the sake of our and God's future, rather than remaining in bondage to closed systems that are considered unchangeable. "Waiting for God to come and remembering the God who has come together create an open attitude toward life as a gift flowing from the past as well as into the future."[9]

This kind of counter-memory, in contrast to the officially authorized version, is wed to a biblically-grounded sense of what justice entails. It is memory work in which the past is more open to public debate, more alive to the unseemly side of a crisis that otherwise is marginalized or denied. This becomes an opening for redemptive grace. It is empowering and transformative. Memory

8. Carter interview on Thom Hartmann program, July 28 2015.

9. Bergmann, "Invoking the Spirit," 173.

poses not the problem of how to connect with the past but how to live out what that remembering actualizes among us—the already-not-yet reality in which we partake.

Some biblical and theological perspectives

Who we are as a people is shaped by remembering biblical stories formed amid the empires of the different periods of biblical history. This in turn can shape how we go about doing what we do as the church in the face of empire today. "Our ancient wisdom tells us to *ask radical questions,* but to *act in the real world.*"[10]

Perspectives from Walter Brueggemann are especially suggestive in this regard.[11] Different perspectives and strategies are emphasized in prophetic books of the Hebrew Bible, corresponding to the respective empires under which the people were living. Ezekiel wrests sovereignty from the powers that had intimidated and abused Israel. "I will make with them a covenant of peace . . . they shall be secure on their own soil; and they shall know that I am the Lord, when I break the bars of their yoke, and save them from the hands of those who enslaved them" (Ezek 34:25, 27). This promise was grounded in a deep theological memory, and summoned the community to respond imaginatively from out of an alternative reality or way of seeing. Jeremiah remembered the wounded and the faithfulness of YHWH, which had a transformative effect on the faith community. Thus, this generated energy and courage to imagine and enact a future that the dominating powers have tried to wipe out. Isaiah 40–55 proclaims the utterance, promise, presence and resolve of YHWH: do not fear the illusions that empire, and its practices and effects evoke. Historical change or liberation will come about, even by means of those seen as enemies, such as the Persian king Cyrus (Isaiah 44). Later, living under the domination of Persia, accommodation and resistance became shrewd intentional strategies, as part of a sustained

10. Lyon, *Silicon Society,* 117.

11. Brueggemann, *Out of Babylon,* 58, 60, 63, 91, 132.

practice of "over-againstness," as passages in Ezra, Nehemiah, Daniel, Esther, and the Joseph stories in Genesis reflect. When Israel fails to remember, to trust in YHWH who alone is ultimate (Is 42:14–16), the empire occupies the vacuum and tries to claim that position for itself.

In the Bible, the numerous calls to remember emerge out of a deep and enduring sense of the relationship between God and humankind. "Israel's life as a covenant community depends on a clear vision and a sharp memory of who God is."[12] God gives birth to us and all that is, saves or liberates from captivity to bondage, and bestows gifts intended not for private gain but for the common good of all. Scripture repeatedly calls us to remember all that God has said and done—particularly for outsiders (Ex 22:2) and slaves (Deut 5:15)—in others words, those who tend to be kept invisible by the dominant powers in a society. Repeated appeals are made to God not to forget but to remember the people and their vulnerability or suffering (Ps 20:3). The Psalmist is audacious in calling God to account: "remember your compassion and love, for they are everlasting" and asks God to "remember me according to your steadfast love and for the sake of your goodness, O Lord" (Ps. 25:6–7). "Rememberers" call on God to remember.

Disappointment and displacement open up space for remembering a God who refuses to abandon the people. We become active subjects, in solidarity with others. YHWH's resolve for the future stands against the facts on the ground. We refuse to succumb to the ways things are, reminded instead that "exile [of whatever kind] is the habitat of the holy."[13] Prophetic poetry dares to insist that there is another reality of hope and new life beyond the empire's control, and invites hearers to walk and shape the world that this opens up. "It authorizes courage, summons defiance, and lines out resistance. . . . In the poetic poetry, YHWH seeks to penetrate the fearful anxiety of Israel, to energize by defying the given and disturbing the presumed world in which the listeners

---

12. Brueggemann, *Truth-telling*, 57.
13. Brueggemann, *Out of Babylon*, 54.

live."[14] Enlivened by the breath of God, we are empowered "to see and resist what betrays God's boundless, unquenchable yearning toward abundant life for all."[15]

Remembering also can be viewed as the fundamental basis for pastoral care in the Bible.[16] God's remembering implies God's movement toward the "object" of God's remembering. Human care and community are possible because we are held in God's memory. Thus, we in turn are to hear and remember one another. Remembering is a form of caring, of making present. To re-member is the opposite of "dis-membering" or forgetting either God or others.

The remembering focus here is much different from self-help and personal adjustment approaches to well-being (cf. 1 Kg 21). The biblical understanding of health involves transformative gestures of solidarity with the marginalized, audacious claims about who really is sovereign, and unexpected interventions in existing arrangements of power. Any pastoral care that shrinks from these matters is likely to be romantic, trivial and irrelevant to the real health issues facing us.[17]

Appropriate forgetting also is important. Repeatedly the appeal is for God to forget, overlook, or forgive what has been done. Because God promises to create a new heaven and earth, what happened before will *not* be remembered, so that there might be a new beginning, or reconciliation. On the one hand, remember where you have come from (Is 51:1–2), but on the other hand, forget in order to enter the new thing God is doing (Is 43:18–19).

Forgetting can be seen as a looking away that makes it possible to begin again. It opens up space for the task of ethical reconfiguration and renewal. Forgetting becomes a means for shifting our perspective, for looking away in order to see. For some who have undergone great trauma, the grip of memory can be unrelenting; they cannot forget. The rawness of memory has the power to inflame. Yet mindful of how malleable memory is, we must

14. Ibid., 55.

15. Moe-Lobeda, *Resisting Structural Evil*, 86.

16. Patton, *Pastoral Care*, 28.

17. Brueggemann, *Out of Babylon*, 24

refuse to give up the work of remembering to those who seek to do so on our behalf, which is why remembering needs to become a deliberate practice.

Writing from a German context in the 1970s, amid the ongoing challenge of coming to grips with the horrors of the Holocaust, Johann Baptist Metz posits that remembering can be seen as the fundamental way of expressing Christian faith. Memory is the inner element of critical consciousness.[18] The "memory of suffering can become, alongside many other often subversive innovative factors in our society, the ferment for that new political life we are seeking on behalf of our future."[19] We remember what interests of empire would prefer that we forget.

The memory of Jesus Christ is a dangerous and liberating memory that continues to question what is reigning over the present and opens up our envisioning and moving into the future. Seen in this way, Christian faith becomes a dangerous, subversive memory, which is at the core of critical consciousness. "Resurrection of the dead" acquires a social-critical function. Christian faith is a dangerous and liberating memory over and against the controls and mechanisms of dominant consciousness and abstract ideals of freedom.[20] Living out this faith—through practices of seeing–remembering–connecting—the church becomes an emancipatory memory. We thus are liberated from all attempts to idolize cosmic and political and economic powers, making them absolute.

Remembering in and through the Eucharist

"Do this in remembrance of me." The Eucharist is located within the biblical context of remembering God's liberation and in-breaking justice. In this meal, resurrection hope is practiced "by connecting the remembrance of God's saving works . . . with our lives."[21] It is a

---

18. Metz, *Faith in History and Society,* 39.

19. Ibid., 118.

20. Ibid, 113, 114.

21. Bieler and Schottroff, *Eucharist,* 163.

practice based on empathy, embodiment and reciprocity between God and human beings, of remembering painful memories and dealing with them in courageous and life-giving ways. At the center of this is the memory of Jesus' death *and* resurrection, bringing to mind his ministry to the poor and sick, and God's saving work through the body of Christ in the world today.

As Andrea Bieler and Luise Schottroff suggest, the remembering (*anamnesis*) of the Eucharist has at least three aspects: (1) God remembers us and we remember God's saving and healing activity in the world, (2) we are drawn into the narrative as involved participants, (3) it embraces all of who we are, the memory itself becoming inscribed in our bodies. Memory involves not just reproducing but re-interpreting "our body memories," our cultural memories and our place memories, all of which are connected through the Eucharist. We participate in the meal as remembering bodies."[22] We bring our bodies to the table with our suppressed and distorted memories, and with the promise that all this is held by God, who remembers. God remembers us and we remember God's saving and healing activity in the world. "Eschatological anamnesis" involves reciprocal activity, anamnetic empathy, and embodied practice.

Margaret Scott makes explicit how the Eucharist is connected with social justice:

> Eucharist is active, it does what it says. It is about change. The Eucharist changes bread and wine, and it changes us. It has a transformative power and hence, the potential for personal and global transformation. There is an energy in the Eucharist that is liberating, making present. As it does, Jesus Christ sets us free—free from personal and national interest; free from greed and the desire for power. We are set free so that we might no longer live just for ourselves. We are liberated from being satisfied with the status quo; liberated to set others free, freed to change the world.[23]

22. Ibid., 174.

23. Scott, *The Eucharist and Social Justice*; from a paper for a course I taught at Lutheran Theoological Seminary in Philadalphia, 2010.

In other words, the Eucharist offers a new way of thinking and acting. Encoded in the Eucharist is a centripetal force that leads us to communion, interdependence and connection with those most different from ourselves. Eucharist makes communion happen. In communion we together eat and drink the body and blood of Christ. We commune with both the divine and the human. We enter into communion with God but also into horizontal communion with people.

William Cavanaugh[24] makes a strong case for how the Eucharist is a counter to the torture (e.g., what Chileans experienced under Pinochet), as well as under other expressions of empire. Torture creates fearful and isolated bodies, docile to the purposes of empire, but Eucharist makes present the body of Christ, a body marked by resistance to worldly power.[25] Eucharist is the church's "counter-politics" to the politics of torture. Torture creates victims, whereas Eucharist creates witnesses. Isolation is overcome, forming a communal body that resists attempts to make victims disappear or become invisible. The Eucharist builds a visible social body capable of resisting domination. If torture is the imagination [of empire], Eucharist is the imagination of the church.[26]

The future reign of God is anticipated, Jesus' conflict with the powers of this world re-membered, and both the future and past dimensions of Christ are brought into the present—as the body of Christ in the world. "[I]n the Eucharist, the Kingdom irrupts into time and 'confuses' the spiritual and the temporal . . . calls the church to be what eschatologically it is . . . living out a vision of what really is real . . . the reign of God disrupting dominating reigns of injustice."[27] Worldly time and space are invaded by the heavenly, resulting in the possibility of a different kind of social practice. We become one with others in the past, present and future: "For as often as you eat this bread and drink this cup, you proclaim the Lord's death until he comes"(1 Cor. 11:26). The fu-

24. Cavanaugh, *Torture and Eucharist.*
25. Ibid., 206.
26. Ibid., 229.
27. Ibid., 206.

ture fulfillment of the past governs the present, oriented by the past and straining toward the future.

8

Subversive Connecting

Connectedness is a sense of being a part of something larger than oneself. It is a sense of belonging, or a sense of accompaniment. It is that feeling in your bones that you are not alone. It is a sense that, no matter how scary things may become, there is a hand for you in the dark. While ambition drives us to achieve, connectedness is the force that urges us to ally, to affiliate, to enter into mutual relationships, to take strength and to grow through cooperative behavior.[1]

Connecting is a key word for what our computers are doing continually, in our Web-based, endlessly interconnected world. But connecting also is a pivotal social practice that is basic to what it means to be human. It is what holds societies together. As earth creatures, we are innately relational and inter-connected, as many biblical references emphasize, beginning with Genesis 2:18 (it is not good that the human be alone). This counters the loneliness and atomization that plague individuals, despite being virtually connected through various social media. We are continually connecting, whether consciously or not. We form friendships and intimate relationships, organize community with those who are nearby neighbors, and well as with those distant from us. It is through connecting that we are able to act and make a difference in the world.

1. Hallowell, "Connectedness," 196.

We also connect what otherwise would remain separate issues or challenges. Connecting results from the kinds of seeing and remembering discussed previously. It occurs because of what is seen and remembered, which motivates and empowers us to move beyond the customary lines that keep us and the challenges separate or unconnected. There are numerous examples of organizing attempts built on making these interconnections today, for example, between climate change, low wages, economic disparities, racism, and how these are exasperated by corporate and political policies that must be changed.

Connecting involves everyday practices that can be a point of entry for what is theologically significant. Such practices are a way of getting at theological substance in ways that are more directly experienced and more readily accessible to people, including those who stand outside any faith tradition. If "seeing" helps people get beyond the illusions, and "remembering" beyond the social amnesia, "connecting" empowers us to move beyond the fear of the other, and into new depths of community, in other words, a connectedness with those who may be most different from ourselves.

Connectedness is closely related to advocacy, public witness and protest; it is what undergirds such. The call for justice can be mere noise in the political system unless it comes from those are connected to the problem and to each other with compassion and intelligence. Communities can move together around problems and opportunities if people are nurtured in their faith to look for God amid the emerging connections. They sense that God is there in the mix, and thus can move toward it hopefully rather than away from it fearfully.

Many kinds of spirituality have long emphasized connectedness. For example, a feminist spirituality is connected to our bodies, to those at the margins, to justice struggles, to particular communities of faith, and to God. It is "the practice of bodily, social, political and personal connectedness so that life comes together in a ways that both transcends and includes the bits and pieces that make up our search for wholeness, freedom, relationship, and full human dignity."[2]

For our purposes here, "subversive connecting" emphasizes connecting that cuts across a) identity markers of race, ethnicity, citizenship, and/or gender, b) religious differences, c) ideological/political differences, d) economic disparities, and e) global power differences. Markers such as these, and the homogeneous communities in which they result, have often been reinforced by religion demarcations that result from colonizing and missionary initiatives. For example, most Indonesian Bataks and African Namibians are assumed to be Lutheran, Hispanics assumed to be Catholic, Arabs assumed to be Muslim. A stable social order, long associated with such markers, typically has been considered to be threatened when these identities or markers are "transgressed" or crossed. This is when connecting becomes subversive.

Fortunately this has been changing. While some communities have become even more economically homogeneous, more and more communities have had to learn to live with greater ethnic and religious diversity in their midst. For example, we currently live in an urban community where as Euro-Americans we often find ourselves in settings where nearly everyone else is Asian, Latino or African-American. In our society, the underlying systemic suspicion, racism, xenophobia, and fear of "the other" continues, occasionally erupting in violent outbursts. The original sin of systemic racism continues to plague our society and world.

Further, many Christian understandings and practices long have been cast in aggressive ways that seek to convert those of other faiths. The "us versus them" dynamic has permeated our ways of seeing and remembering, which thus blocks the kinds of connecting that is much deeper than *tolerating* "the other" and that can lead to more authentic community across such markers. A much more radical sense of connecting and of community is at the heart of the theological understandings and practices envisioned here.

There needs to be more systemic connecting across what too often have been approached as separate if not competing issues

2. Russell, *Church in the Round*, 187.

or challenges. For example, this began to occur some decades ago in the early stages of a mostly white environmental movement. Still today "African-Americans are more likely to live near environmental hazards like power plants and be exposed to hazardous air pollution, including higher levels of nitrogen oxides, ozone, particulate matter and carbon dioxide than their white counterparts. Environmental injustices are taking black lives—that's why our fight for equality has to include climate and environmental justice too."[3]

Inter-connections between the different challenges we face today are crucial, for the sake of more adequate understanding and for responding more effectively to issues. Many movements today are making important efforts to connect people and issues. Gender, age, superstitious cultural traditions, poverty and environment pollution are often interconnected.

For example, in a rural African village, there was an alarming upsurge in the number of older women being killed. With their red eyes, they were suspected of being witches who were killing off the children. The women's eyes were red from cooking with cow dung in enclosed huts without adequate ventilation, dangerously polluting the air, and bringing early death to children. With new cooking stoves and fuels, both the women and children are no longer dying but beginning to thrive. Injustices that often have been viewed separately must be addressed in such interconnected ways if they are to be redressed effectively.

If the basic question asked from a biblical justice commitment is "what's wrong with the whole picture?" then it is essential that the whole picture be put together, rather than addressing the parts separately. With today's climate justice challenges such interconnections have become global even cosmic in nature. We continually need to ask who is not "at the table" when perspectives on issues are discussed, and take measures to assure that this is corrected.

"Connecting" goes to the root of the words "religion" and "*ligo*"—rebinding or reconnecting broken bonds or relationships.

3. Ellison and Jones, "Pollution Isn't Colorblind," par. 1.

To act religiously in the world involves "rebinding the broken cosmos,"[4] healing or mending of what is broken, separated, alienated. It is implied in the Hebraic notions of *shalom* and *tikkun olam*. It is humanity's shared responsibility to heal, repair and transform the world. From different faith perspectives, this is a connecting that brings in something new and different—a new reality with persons and realities seemingly quite different, even foreign from each other. It thus embodies a radicality that refuses to stay away from differences but is actually transformed through and by them.

Christ and connectedness

According to the Gospels, connecting with disparate people is what Jesus regularly was doing—with those considered culturally "unclean," despised, rejected by those whom society considered upstanding and respectable. Jesus reached out to those whose social status had impoverished them and their possibilities for social connections, who were removed from family or community. This also included a rich tax collector, Zaccheus. Women, the poor, those of questionable reputations or occupations were again and again sought out by Jesus. As he said, "when you give a banquet, invite the poor, the crippled, the lame and the blind" (Luke 14:13). Most radically of all, rather than operating with the assumption that some are "enemies," Jesus instructed his followers, "Love your enemies, do good to those who hate you" (Luke 6:27).

"What made Christ persuasive was his radical non-fearful love for others."[5] He restored social connections that had been cut off, but without repeating the logic of power-over possession, without trying to control those he encountered. He was willing to be with people, to connect deeply with them, to empower without dominating. And it is practices such as these that made him subversive, a threat to the powers dominating people, who depended on instilling fear. He was "systematically undercutting the fear on

4. Schultze, *Habits*, 72.
5. Kotsko, *Politics of Redemption*, 199.

which power depends by undoing the divisions that keep people suspicious and vulnerable"[6]

A primary function of crucifixion (or more subtle means for getting rid of someone) has been to deter future "rebels," to warn them if they do not go along with the reigning powers that this too could happen to them. This also occurs in religiously-based institutions. Going along with the mandates of the reigning powers is the ongoing temptation. For many this is necessary for their livelihood or survival. But being followers of Christ means refusing such temptations based on fear, and instead, restoring or making often unpopular connections.[7] This is likely to be considered by leaders to be threatening, not sufficiently subservient. Instead, it is subversive of the reigning powers.

Connectedness is grounded in the Triune God

Connecting is grounded deeply and fundamentally in who God is, not as an autonomous, hierarchical monarch reigning over and dominating over others, but as a God who is intrinsically relational, i.e., trinitarian. The resurgence of trinitarian theology has been one of the significant theological developments of the past half century. In the 1970s this was just beginning, but since then Juergen Moltmann, Leonard Boff, Catherine LaCugna and a host of others have inspired many others who have raised the significance of conceiving God in trinitarian terms without losing the distinctiveness of each "person." The three are in communion with each other, in a differentiated plurality.

"The Trinity is about God's life with us and our life with each other."[8] *Perichoresis* refers to the dynamic mutual indwelling, the inter-penetrating, permeating interaction (dance) within the Triune God. This becomes grounds for challenging hierarchical patterns of subordination, domination and individualism in hu-

6. Ibid., 201.

7. Ibid., 203.

8. LaCugna, *God for Us*, 1.

man society. "The Trinity corresponds to a community in which people are defined through their relations with one another and in the significance for one another, not in opposition to one another, in terms of power and possession."[9] Domination of one over the other violates the nature of God and of human beings. God exists for, with and through the other. In contrast, a nontrinitarian theology of God can open the door to every kind of ideology and idolatry.[10]

For example, Nigerian Lutheran theologian Ibrahim Bitrus calls for re-contextualizing the divine and human African community according to God's gift of triune community: "The Triune God's *perichoretic* ways of communing and transforming humanity and all of creation free and empower Nigerians to accompany the Triune God in liberating the Nigeria from its systemic problems."[11]

Relation is at the heart of who God is. The Trinity reminds us that deepening connectedness or relationality with all of creation is at the heart of divine, human, and cosmic realities. "The church cannot participate in the triune fellowship of God without also sharing in God's own participation in the world's suffering, godforsakenness and death." Participating in and deeply connecting with the world, "is the only way for the church to be itself."[12]

This kind of connectedness and reciprocity profoundly contradicts prevailing cultural assumptions, and the rivalries, animosities, and violent competition to which separateness leads. This deepens rather than bridging religious, racial, gender and ethnic fissures. In contrast, we are unconditionally connected with God and thus with each other. God in Christ chooses our neighbors for us, connecting them with us as brothers and sisters, in a way that transcends time and space and every identity boundary. Practices such as deep connecting inevitable puts the church in tension if not conflict with adversarial dynamics in any culture. The truth

9. Moltmann, *Trinity and the Kingdom,* 198.

10. LaCugna, *God for Us,* 395.

11. Bitrus, "The Significance of the New Trinitarian Hermeneutics," 266.

12. Lewis, *Between Cross and Resurrection,* 346, 347.

is revealed that we model the image of God's triune community as interconnected, related persons in community. Original sin is the self-deluding desire to deny this connectedness[13] or deep solidarity.

> Liturgy affects a transfiguration of our lives. It enacts the presence of the Holy Spirit in the church, and world and all of creation, understood as participating in the historic economy of the trinitarian life of God. It invites human beings to participate with Jesus Christ, who has already carried out humanity into the Godhead, in the divine dance. This participation gives us new eyes to see the world and new energy to bear witness to it."[14]

As in other theological works today, this sense of deep connectedness permeates the recent papal encylical, *Laudato Si*. "Everything is interconnected, and this invites us to develop a spirituality of global solidarity which flows from the mystery of the Trinity."[15] Although publicized as addressing especially the environmental crisis, the encyclical throughout points to the interconnections with various other social, economic and political factors, particularly as they affect those most vulnerable. "The ecclesial conversion needed to bring about lasting change is also a community conversion."[16]

What is noteworthy is how secular climate justice activists are connecting with this church document. For example, Naomi Klein was invited to speak at a special Vatican conference where she stated, "The growing understanding [that we can shift to a more stable climate and fairer economy *at the same time*] is why you are seeing some surprising and even unlikely alliances. Like, for instance, me [a secular Jew] at the Vatican. Like trade unions, Indigenous, faith and green groups working more closely together than ever before."[17]

13. Ibid., 350.
14. Best and Robra, *Costly Obedience*, 67.
15. Francis, *Laudato Si,* par. 240.
16. Ibid., par. 219.
17. Klein, "People and Planet First," par. 18.

As Klein later reflected,

> A millennia-old engine designed to proselytize and
> convert non-Christians is now preparing to direct its
> missionary zeal inward, challenging and changing foun-
> dational beliefs about humanity's place in the world
> among the already faithful. People of . . . missionary
> faiths, believe deeply in something that a lot of secular
> people aren't so sure about: that all human beings are
> capable of profound change. They remain convinced that
> the right combination of argument, emotion and experi-
> ence can lead to life-altering transformations . . . And
> if that happens—if transformation is as contagious as it
> seems to be here—well, we might just stand a chance of
> tackling climate change.[18]

The connectedness of catholicity

Catholicity denotes the connectedness and universality of the
whole church (not only the Roman Catholic).[19] Catholicity re-
sides in Christ himself and is what follows from the church being
Christ's body in the world, in conformity with the Crucified One.
A church of the cross "is related to the whole and is catholic in so
far as . . . it seeks and restores the lost, rejected and oppressed"[20]
The church is truly catholic insofar as it exists not for its own sake
but for the whole world. The church yearns for the whole world to
be redeemed, reconciled, or fulfilled at the close of the age.[21]

Diversity becomes the matrix in which the gift of the church's
catholicity takes shape. This goes far beyond multiculturalism or
pluralism or tolerance. It is appreciated not primarily through
theological concepts but through shared life experiences across
all that divides us. The *character* of our communities and the

---

18. Klein, "A Radical Vatican," par. 47–50.
19. Lewis, *Between Cross and Resurrection*, 348.
20. Moltmann, *Church in the Power*, 352.
21. Ibid., 365.

power inequities within and between them become theologically significant.[22]

Catholicity also points to the totality of the human race as its final fulfillment.[23] Historically this usually has been applied in hierarchical, triumphalistic ways, in conquering colonizing and missionary attempts to bring all people under the sway of Christ, and thus of the church. This must continue to be challenged, as many post-colonial theologians have been doing. But there also is a sense in which catholicity points to the inter-connected totality of all human beings and creation, which crosses religious and all kinds of other boundaries.

In this sense, as Alan Lewis suggests, the church catholic embodies "a subversion of and a proleptic deliverance from the pathological individualism, polarization, and sectionalism of our terminal society."[24] Connectedness and reciprocity (grounded in the Trinity) profoundly contradict prevailing cultural assumptions. Instead of individualism and polarization due to differences, we are unconditionally connected: God chooses our neighbors for us. We are connected with them as brothers and sisters, not just theoretically or idealistically, but in a way that transcends time and space and every identity boundary. Actually practicing such connecting sets the church in conflict with culture. The truth is revealed that we model the image of God's triune community as connected, related persons in community. Sin is exposed in the self-deluding desire to deny this connectedness.

The connectness of communio

Communio goes back to New Testament perspectives of the church, where the related word, *koinonia*, is especially prominent. Since then, it has had a long and complex history, reflecting how it has developed in different Christian traditions.

22. Albrecht, *Character of Our Communities.*

23. Lewis, *Between Cross and Resurrection,* 356.

24. Ibid., 350.

For example, Martin Luther uses *communion sanctorum* to refer not only to the gathering of the people of God *(ecclesia)* but also the dynamic of participation in Christ, and with one another. Through the sacrament we become organically interconnected so that we are "changed into one another."

> The sacrament has no blessing and significance unless loves grow daily and so changes a person that he is made one with all others. For just as the bread is made out of many grains ground and mixed together, and out of the bodies of many grains there comes the body of the bread . . . and through the interchange of his blessings and our misfortunes, we become one loaf, one bread, one body, one drink, and have all things in common. . . . In this way we are changed into one another and are made into a community by love.[25]

Through the activity of the Holy Spirit, God indwells and empowers inter-subjectivity. *Communio* becomes an embodied sign of the connectedness or interdependence of all of life. It is a divine gift, not an imperative. We are freed from being obsessed with "doing right," which can work against and destroy community. Yet we are also implicated in a calling, to live out this reality in our life together.

This comes alive in the wonderfully diverse congregation in which we worshiped for over a decade in Geneva, Switzerland. Here people from around the world regularly gather around the Table of Holy Communion—there to glimpse a vision of the feast to come. People from around the world bring their different pieties, practices and beliefs, extend hospitality to the constant flow of strangers, shed tears of grief and compassion with each other, sing songs from cultures around the world, and together pray the Lord's Prayer in many languages. Here God's *communio* is glimpsed and experienced, as the pulsating life of the Spirit flows in and through the people who are the body of Christ, the communion of saints, strangers and sojourners united across bounds

---

25. Luther, "The Blessed Sacrament of the Holy and True Body of Christ, and the Brotherhoods, 1519" in *Luther's Works*, 35:58.

of class, races, culture, nationality, and yes, even religion. At the baptism of a young man whose mother is a Finnish Lutheran and father an Afghan Hindu, he heard from the pastor that being baptized into the Christian family did not mean renouncing his Hindu family roots.

How pivotal *communio* is for moving beyond the illusions, amnesia and individualism that pervade so much of the world today. This became far more evident to me during the years I directed theological work of the Lutheran World Federation. Especially since 1990, the LWF has defined itself as "a *communion* of churches which confess the Triune God, agree in the proclamation of the Word of God and are united in pulpit and altar fellowship. Through Word and sacraments every local church is bound into the wider communion of churches."[26] Moving beyond these general platitudes, *communio* is lived out as those in member churches of this communion advocate and act out of this sense of relatedness, responsibility, accountability to others in the communion, and through them, to the rest of the created world.

What it means to be formed as *communio* and to live this out in the world, inevitably sets us in tension with many of the assumptions, logic and outcomes of neoliberalism, which in its continual quest for what is economically profitable and efficient, tends to weaken those very bonds of family and community that theologically are constitutive of who we are.

North American church life, priorities and practices are often perceived quite differently by those from elsewhere. To hear that, we need to listen and move beyond the polite levels of being a *communio*, to more honest levels of interaction. This kind of interaction began occurring in a 2010 online course I taught through the Lutheran Theological Seminary at Philadelphia. One of the participants, the head of a seminary in Madagascar, decried the blatant corruption of the government in which his church had also been caught up, and as the Americans in the class were decrying the effects of the economic recession, he quietly commented, "I haven't been paid at all for nearly a year." Also, a white Australian

26. Constitution of the Lutheran World Federation (1990), Article III.

Lutheran pastor, training poor illiterate Aboriginal pastors in central Australia, heard from one of these pastors: "God must love white fellas better, I betcha." He went on to recount how Lutheran missionaries who had come to them many years ago had never translated the Old Testament (other than the Psalms) into indigenous languages. The Aboriginal people were not exposed to the more prophetic calling of the church. This was not remembered, so that it could be connected critically with the blatant suffering and deprivation they currently were experiencing and beginning to express aloud. Blatant realities of suffering in other parts of the world not only put what we are experiencing in perspective, but provoke new dimensions of global solidarity.

Communio has significant implications for how we are formed morally, for the expanse of our moral vision, for how we deliberate over our differences, and for the scope of our action, which needs to account for the significant power differences within a global communion As the 2003 Assembly of the LWF stated,

> Our mutual participation in Christ leads us to challenge all those cultural, economic and political forces that define and tend to divide us. Thus, communion can make us uncomfortable as assumptions and practices that we take for granted are challenged and we are pushed to consider questions that we would not as separate churches on our own. These tensions, which can at times be threatening, are also a sign of vitality; they can deepen the realization of what it means to be a communion. We give thanks to God that our communion is blessed with diversity.[27]

The connectedness that is reconciliation

On occasions, such diversity opens up entrenched differences that cannot be covered over but must be faced, and provokes the need for reconciliation.

27. LWF, "Message of the Tenth Assembly," 4.

Reconciliation is a gift of God in this world, and must become a central practice of the church in society. [28] Mission, evangelism or diaconia cannot simply be added to churches constructed on the basis of individualistic piety and consumer religion. Too many congregations are fashioned on a model of privilege, exclusion and prosperity. The church must be liberated from the limitations imposed by individualism and functionalism, from being reduced to another organization competing for power and influence, and complicit in the current ideological warfare of society. [29] We must discern how God in Christ—the Word made flesh— resists all competing ideologies in our world today.

Assimilation models of church (become "like us") tend to prevail over reconciliation. In radical reconciliation, people are being transformed by the reality of the other. Even congregations that are more racially or ethnically diverse do not necessarily experience reconciliation, because the cultural tone and practices have been established by those who were first there.

In contrast, most first century congregations really were multicultural—diverse mixtures of Jews and those from other cultures. Paul and those working with him went first to the Jews and then to the Gentiles. Together these congregations produced a movement for social unity across divides of culture, tradition, class and race. "Ultimately, the unity of the first-century church was the result of the miracle of reconciliation—a conversion from their ethnocentrism to the intention, practice and vision of Jesus."[30] They were also colonized people, living under the Roman Empire. In such congregations, those who were colonized worshipped alongside those who were agents of their colonizing oppressors. It was quite a subversive practice, to invite agents of the empire into these faith communities that were largely constituted by Jews. The oppressed ethnic group (Jews) was actually welcoming the dominant ruling group into their midst, not out of civil politeness but because of the radicality of what reconciliation was about. Those with privi-

28. Schmeichen, *Christ the Reconciler,* 144.

29. Ibid, 86, 140.

30. deYoung, et al, *United by Faith,* 37

lege were invited into their community in a remarkable strategy of inclusion.

What did liberation for both groups mean? Loyalty to the practices of empire was replaced with an "in Christ" consciousness, and with practices reflecting such. Those with power and influence in the empire actually defected from their status, exchanging places with those of little privilege or power. If the centurion Cornelius (Acts 10:48) could be drawn into a new circle of belonging, then the implications for being subversive toward the claims of the Roman state were revolutionary.[31] The more Cornelius experienced communion with people who were oppressed, the more he was internally drawn by the Holy Spirit to challenge the claims of the Roman state. Such connecting was intrinsic in what the gospel was about.

Status inversion and subversion of the social order occurred in the early churches. These were generally begun by those who were Jewish. Thus, by becoming part of these faith communities, Romans and Greeks were identifying with a socially stigmatized people, connecting with those oppressed by Rome, which had life-altering repercussions for both groups. Gentiles were learning what marginalization within the empire meant. This also affected class and gender relations. Women, oppressed because of both their gender and colonized status, were considered doubly subversive.

Connecting goes beyond established polarities

Contemporary interpreters of what was going in New Testament writings are especially helpful here. Birgitte Kahl points out that the antithesis of "Jews versus Christians" embedded a deadly enemy construct into the core of justification theology, and must be corrected today. In his letter to the Galatians, Paul was opposing law as embodied in and enforced by the Roman Empire, rather than Jewish law (Torah). At the heart of Paul's theological claim

31. Jenning, *Christian Imagination*, 269.

is not a polarity of Jews versus Gentiles, nor any other polarity. His radically new insight is that "in Christ" the dichotomies of the current world order are invalidated, such as hierarchical polarities that juxtapose self and other, good and evil, righteous and unrighteous, and, we might add today, Christians versus those of another (or no) faith. These vanish in the radically new practice of becoming "one" *with* another, rather than one *against* the Other.[32]

Historically, because how "being in Christ" was subsequently used (especially since Constantine) in a conquering way over others, the freshness of this Pauline insight was soon lost. Whether it can be retrieved today, perhaps through different expressions, is an open question, given how off-putting the "in Christ" language has been to those who are not confessing Christians.

Martin Luther did not pick up on this in his time, largely because of his adversarial stance toward all those opposing his reformation efforts. In our time, not only must we denounce the deplorable antagonisms that resulted, but insist that *solidarity across such boundaries is at the heart of the gospel*. It is from such a stance of solidarity, rather than from entrenched and often vicious political polarization, that more effective address of today's crises can be addressed more effectively.

As stated in the theses of the Radicalizing Reformation project: "For Paul, the justice of God implies . . . that "in Christ" the polarities and hierarchies of this "present evil world order"(Gal 1:4) have been overcome. "We" are not what segregates us from the "others" but what interconnects us with them. The human divisions of nation, religion, gender, and class, which constitute the "self" as enemy and rival of the "other," are removed in baptism "like old garments." A new praxis of becoming "one" through mutuality and solidarity creates a new form of being human—and a new world (Gal 6:2.15). "God's justice, the justification of the human being, and human justice are all inseparably connected."[33]

A challenge Paul faced was that of reorganizing the faith community in ways that were not hierarchical, antagonistic, or

32. Kahl, *Galatians Re-Imagined.*
33. Radicalizing Reformation, thesis 59.

exclusive, but instead, with mutuality and solidarity. Rather than being competitive and combative toward others,[34]both Jews and Gentiles were included. Those to whom Paul's letter was addressed participated in and to some extent benefited from Roman rule, but the order underlying this imperial system was being challenged or subverted. What emerges in God's "new creation" is a new "self-with-the-other" (rather than over-and-against the other). "The old self is co-crucified and resurrected through the power of self-less mutuality, solidarity and compassion."[35] Through "the 'birth-canal' of divine self-othering at the cross", humans are remade in the image of God, rather than as a self that conquers and consumes others."[36] Solidarity with the weak and despised "other" embodies the new order, which begets a new and transformed humanity. That is the ecclesial calling for today, in ways that are bound to be subversive of what is dominating us now.

Forming communities of discernment

Today we are formed in communion with God and others, in ways that call for faithful responses in relation to those whose lived realities are quite different from our own. We may not even be able to assume that others share our assumptions or ways of interpreting Scripture. Yet we are held together by God in Christ through the Holy Spirit in ways that enable us to talk together about our different ways of seeing or interpreting, without this degenerating into shouting matches, power plays, or mere restatements of our own positions. We are pulled into one another's' realities and seek to understand such more deeply. Simplistic condemnations of the positions of the other will not suffice.

Therefore, any process of common discernment necessarily requires humility and care, not only to avoid giving unnecessary offense, but because *how* we interact with one another, especially

34. Kahl, 269–70.
35. Ibid., 269.
36. Ibid., 289.

across all the disparities that divide us, itself bears witness to the interactive body of Christ in the world. There may be enormous power disparities, advantages and disadvantages among us, yet we deeply yearn to be connected, as parts of the one body of Christ. Together the different parts are constitutive of the catholicity of the body. Thus, it is not a matter of some correcting others out of a sense of "one-up-man-ship" or dominating power over them, as often occurs in competitive verbal debates that are preoccupied with who will "win." Instead, the attention here is on what can be added or complemented from our respective differing perspectives. How contributions are offered can be as important as is the content of what is said. Finding connections amid our differences is pivotal.

In the kind of communal discernment suggested here, the wisdom of all is required. Discernment involves eyes, ears, mind, heart, bodies, experiences, feelings, stories, histories and more. What is especially crucial is honoring what is seen or remembered by those who often are left out. Far more is at stake than a renewing of minds, understood in a narrow sense. Discernment does not mean knowing for sure; that kind of confidence can lead to dangerous hubris. Active discernment necessarily occurs in community with others, which helps to keep us humble. It involves plunging deeply into seeing and remembering realities of those who are most different from us. Through such solidarity with them, how we see, feel and evaluate our faith and ethical convictions begins to be transformed. This is a pivotal aspect of what it means to be and to grow together as a communion. In such a communion, the process of deliberation for the sake of discernment is more important that coming up with a finished statement. What is crucial is not speaking, but listening, being transformed by the other and living this out through our commitments and actions, in other words, *enacting* communion, not just talking about it.

A sense of this occurred in the work of the diverse task force appointed in 1990 to develop the ELCA social statement on abortion.[37] The task force included a wide spectrum: from a doctor who

37. ELCA, "Abortion."

regularly performed abortions and others who with her strongly affirmed the right of a woman to choose, as well as those who were strongly opposed to such and actively organizing against such. It included those who counseled especially poor women of color with unwanted pregnancies, as well as theological ethicists and public policy activists. When they first came together, to me as the staff director, it was palpable how much they perceived those with opposing commitments as "enemies." This of course was being reinforced by how the "pro-life" vs. "pro-choice" battle lines permeated public life and separated people in the wider church and society.

The first meeting began by sharing personal experiences that had especially influenced individuals' different positions on abortion. With this, some of the barriers between them began to be chipped away. The aim was not to "win over" opponents through argument, intimidation or sheer numbers but to understand their differences more deeply and to broaden the common ground among them. When some consciously attempted to articulate positions that were quite different from their own, it felt like a rare holy moment. In the process that ensued, those in "opposing camps" continued getting to know and pray for one another. In a prayer at the closing Eucharist, one of the women thanked God for one of the men with whom she often disagreed, because she could argue with him as she did with her own brother, knowing that in Christ they are together in one family.

What was key in this process is that task force members worked from central convictions that they shared (e.g., "human life in all phases of its development is God-given and has intrinsic value, worth, and dignity"), and from there, moved outward to areas where they disagreed. Here they deliberated until they found agreement on what they could say together, and left certain questions open for persons to make responsible decisions that were contextually variable and in that sense "catholic."

The final statement cut across the usual "pro-life" and "pro-choice" lines so entrenched in society. After it finally was adopted by the church-wide assembly, the public media and others failed in trying to characterize it according to the usual prevailing categories. Yet it has continued to remain as the widely-affirmed position of the ELCA for over twenty-five years, guiding difficult personal and public policy decisions. This was a pivotal time in which the ELCA gave public witness to what it means for the church, empowered by the Spirit, to become a community of moral deliberation.

When we are compelled to relate and connect with each other in deeper, theologically-grounded ways, we are freed to distance ourselves sufficiently from assumptions to which we cling, in order to be able to change what we value. Values we hold in common can bring us together, rather than values driving us apart. The mutual confirmation by one another of our deeply-held values leads eventually to an enhanced sense of community and of the common good—by talking through difficult issues, not avoiding them. This cannot be imposed from above but takes shape in the space of our relationality with each other, as empowered participants in a deliberative process rather than passive recipients of a final product.

In the give-and-take process, and the resulting deeper connecting, there can be a ferreting out of ideological assumptions of those who differ, as we together search for what is faithful to what God intends. We need what the experience and insights of what others can bring, so that through them the "otherness" of biblical or other texts might speak in new ways to us. In the process, our sense of "we" is bound to be transformed; we can no longer think of "us" in ways that stand against "others." It is through this that a more authentic and credible public position is likely to emerge, one that incorporates a variety of perspectives and thus is pluralistic rather than monolithically driven by ideological differences.

Differences are constitutive of unity or connectedness that is theologically grounded, for the sake of the world.

9

Ecclesia for the Sake of the World

Many have reflected on the implications of being the church today, under what have been identified as marks of the church: "one, holy, catholic and apostolic"(Nicene Creed). For example, Craig Nessan revisits these marks as they motivate practices for exercising ethical responsibility in the world: "oneness" authorizes practices of reconciliation and peacemaking, "holiness" summons advocacy for just structures that provide for all, "catholicity" places us in solidarity with all that God has created, and "apostolicity" sends us forth to respect and defend the dignity of all.[1] As Peter Schmiechen sums it up, "To confess One Holy Catholic Church is to point to the embodiment of reconciliation as a gift of God in this world."[2] As Hans-Peter Grosshans puts it, when people profess to "believe" in the "one holy catholic apostolic Church," they are expressing "their trust in the church as the earthly space . . . opened by the truth of the gospel, where the people of God live out the reconciliation, peace and justice that is the inbreaking of God's realm, intended to draw in all of humankind and creation."[3]

What I have been developing throughout this book builds upon understandings such as these. Further, I am proposing that because of the inevitably subversive mission to which God most centrally is calling us today—as uncovered through

1. Nessan, *Shalom Church,* 173.

2. Schmeichen, 144.

3. Grosshans, *One Holy Catholic Apostolic Church,* 14.

seeing–remembering–connecting—the boundaries of the church need to be viewed in more flexible, less institutionalized, more expansive ways that they usually have been. "Wherever God acts in a liberating way in and through human beings . . . and others are drawn into that process . . . there 'church' appears in the full sense of the word."[4]

"The church becomes more itself the more it loses power."[5] In the process of its usual institutional trappings and supports being peeled away, the church may seem to become less definable. It may become a less distinct institution, but at the same time, is both more worldly and more otherworldly. It becomes more transcendent of what is dominating or ruling in society today by becoming more engaged (more immanent) with what actually is occurring in society, world and creation.

Beyond the usual institutional entrapments of "church"

Many of the shortfalls of how the church relates to society today were identified in the first chapter. Seeing–remembering–connecting is at the heart of what Christian faith as a set of practices has long been about, and also is in tension with the institutional church mantra, "let's get back on the track to numerical and institutional success."

With reference to major heresies in church history, Stephen Pickard refers to the "Docetic ecclesial heresy" when an anxious church resorts to top-down, non-collaborative, tightly controlled ministry and leadership. "Pelagian ecclesial heresy" occurs when an anxious church loses a sense of its transcendent identity, and obsessively focuses instead on efficient processes, rationalizing resources, strategic planning, and measurable outcomes.[6]

---

4. Soelle, *Thinking About God*, 137–138.
5. Soelle, *Silent Cry*, 288.
6. Pickard, *Seeking the Church*, 76–77.

The church is called to live out the biblical witness as centered in Jesus Christ. This necessitates a posture of vulnerability and openness to the world, rather than measuring its institutional strength by the size of membership, finances, buildings and programs. This does not imply dwelling on its weakness or survival, which can become an internal obsession of the church. Instead, faithfulness is in terms of intentionally and consistently resisting systemic domination, and engaging and seeking to transform what actually is going on in the world. This mission of God for the sake of the world is central to what the church is called to be about, rather than institutional survival. Rather than this being an idealistic platitude that can sound out-of-touch with the real practical implications of being church, the refocusing here through the framework of seeing–remembering–connecting might lead toward a new flourishing of the church in society for the sake of all creation.

Because of the institutional baggage typically associated with the word "church," a shift in focus and language may be needed. As articulated by the Centre for Living Christianity in Edinburgh:

> Many people today feel an instant disconnect or disinterest in 'institutional' or 'organised' religion. There is a sense abroad that faith, not least Christian faith, has been turned into a self-perpetuating bureaucracy which operates out of self-interest, refuses difficult questions, and suppresses lternatives . . . Can we break free of institutionalisation, and redo our structures according to a vision of hope in a broken world? Can we hold inherited and emerging church in creative tension?"[7]

Vitor Westhelle describes today's "Babylonian captivity" of the church that entraps it, on the one hand, to inner institutional formation, and on the other hand, to assimilation into the politico-cultural order.

> The challenge to the church calls for liberation from this double captivity: either being obsessed by its own home economics and keeping its house in order and its books

7. Centre for Living Christianity, Website introduction.

solvent, or adjusting itself to the whims of the regime of the day. . . . If the church loses its identity to either or both of these, the church displays its captivity either as idolatry or as demonry. Idolatry results from being obsessively preoccupied with its own house, whereas not having a public voice is a manifestation of the symptoms of demonic possession, being rendered mute, incapable of having an authentic public voice.[8]

By using "*ecclesia,*" I am suggesting the need to go back to the original meaning of "church" which was based on the Greek notion of *ecclesia,* designating the public assembly of free (male) citizens of a Greek city state, called together to speak freely and deliberate publicly on matters of life and justice in their city.[9] When the Greek city states found their governments had become too corrupt and oppressive, they would call for an *ecclesia,* an assembly outside the civil authority of the city. If enough people came out and refused to accept the existing centralized civil authority, that government would collapse. In the New Testament, Paul drew upon and further developed this theologically to refer to the church as the new community created in and through Jesus Christ.

What is important for our purposes here is to realize how closely the original intent of *ecclesia*—"the power of persons in community to influence their corporate lives and the world for good and ill,"[10]—is strikingly similar to what is occurring in many movements today that are resisting powers of domination or "business as usual." The clear objective is to put democratic processes in the hands of the people. This dynamic is also occurring in religious life. Here is where churches that have come from the Reformation should be especially well-suited. But "the priesthood of all believers" has more often become a Protestant slogan rather than what actually activates this kind of movement.

Ecclesia here is a "place" or "event" of seeing, remembering and connecting, of putting together what is fragmentary, pointing

8. Westhelle, "The Priesthood of All Believers," 179.

9. Fredrickson, "Free Speech in Pauline Political Theology," 346.

10. Fredrickson, "Pauline Ethics," 116.

to what is true, enabling us to see and act, including in organized actions with others. It implies the long-term challenge of nurturing and organizing communities of resistance against the dominant scripts and the injustices they entail—as was much of the New Testament church in its struggle in the midst of empire. These communities today are intentionally collaborative across boundaries of religion, geography and self-interest.

Through common practices—such as preaching, teaching, celebrating, caring, community-formation, and organizing—the church as *ecclesia* begins to counter the illusion, amnesia, and disconnectedness, in other words, the sin, bondage, blindness, a-historicity, and privatization that enable the powers of domination to prevail. In addition to recognizable practices, such as proclaiming the Word and celebrating the sacraments, this also evokes expressions that are more porous and publicly accessible to others, including those who have had minimal religious connections. This involves crossing some of the usual boundaries between sacred and secular, between "us" and "them," between local and global realities, between Christians and those of other faiths, between racial/ethnic or other affinity groups, between humans and the rest of nature, in ways that are trans-contextual, transfigurational and thus transformative[11]—for the sake of the world that God creates, loves, redeems and continually transforms.

This means questioning some of the boundaries we typically have associated with "church," in ways that intersect with other faiths, or organizations that may not be faith-based but are also focused on the common good. Amazingly, even Luther in the sixteenth century was suggestive here! According to his interpretation of Genesis, God built for Adam a "temple." "The tree of the knowledge of good and evil was Adam's church, altar and pulpit . . . somewhat like a chapel in which there were many trees of the same variety . . . "[12] This radically inclusive (i.e., catholic) view of the church includes all humans (all were Adam's descendants) "who would have gathered on the Sabbath day . . . where trees were

---

11. Blooomquist, "Lutheran Theology in the Future," 200–203.

12. *Luther's Works*, 1:95.

planted in large number."[13] This imagery includes creation itself. Westhelle postulates that, going beyond Luther, this multiplicity portends the diversity of religions and their different forms of worship and organization. This is consistent with Luther's sense of the multi-center character of the church. Every "tree of life" offers sustenance and living space for different communities—places for worship and discernment.[14]

Brian McLaren describes the liberating, transformative, subversive church as characterized by (a) companionship (*with* others), (b) conviviality (living *together*) and (c) conspiracy (*against* powers of domination). Such a church seeks to overthrow hostilities, oppositions, exclusions and fears, and instead plots together with others for goodness. "This is what I imagine Jesus, Moses, the Buddha and Mohammed doing if they met one another on the road."[15] This is a "with-ness" that accompanies and affirms others rather seeking to convert them. Christ does not belong to any religion for God has already offered Christ as a gift to the world (John 3:16).

What might this imply for ecclesial leadership formation and support?

The preceding chapters have set forth a framework for how churches (and other faith communities) and their relationship to society might be conceived differently. Thus, it is intended to provoke conversation and creative action in different contexts, rather than providing a prescriptive set of "how to's." Yet this seeing–remembering–connecting framework does suggest important shifts in how theological education (leadership formation) is conceived and structured, and how faith communities (e.g., congregations) and ministries are supported and sustained.

13. Ibid.: 105.
14. Westhelle, "Priesthood of All Believers," 181.
15. McLaren, *Why Did Jesus*, 231.

This implies re-conceiving what theological education has been about and how it is pursued. Some of these shifts are already occurring, such as through Theological Education for Emerging Ministries (TEEM) and various efforts to provide theological education by extension and/or online, especially for those in other careers. These increasingly are the trends, such that soon only a minority of those entering the ordained ministry will have gone through traditional in-residence seminary formation.

Going further, the framework of seeing–remembering–connecting suggests departing from the usual ways of organizing theological education curricula. It is based on the key premises that church and ministry are thoroughly (a) collaborative, interactive, permeating, even *perichoretic* (see previous chapter) and (b) for the sake of God's mission of justice in the world. Notice that *perichoresis*, inspired by thinking about the Triune God, goes much deeper than collaboration, into a radical mutuality or deep solidarity with the other. If this becomes more central in what formation is for, rather than primarily preparing individual leaders to be effective in sustaining and growing congregations as institutional silos set off from and in competition with one another, then theological education needs to be shaped and operate quite differently.

"Seeing" implies that formation *begins* not by engaging the texts (biblical, theological, historical, etc.) but engaging the contexts, and the varied experiences students bring, and learning to see in deeper more critical ways what is going on there. This contrasts with the more superficial ways of seeing that typically prevail in society. "Remembering" is where traditional texts and insights are engaged deeply, intentionally opened up (and "transfigured") in relation to what is being "seen" so that it really becomes engaging, rather remaining abstract and theoretical. If the collaborative nature of what it means to be the church for the sake of the world is to be embodied and lived out, then practices of connecting (with those in the church, with outsiders, with those of other faiths, other disciplines, other movements and organizations, etc.) become much more strategic.

Rather that organized according to what have been the usual theological disciplines, this necessarily occurs in pervasively interdisciplinary ways throughout a curriculum. It goes against the grain of how those who teach in theological education are usually credentialed (with a doctorate in a theological field). It means drawing those with other areas of expertise into this formation process, as fully collaborative partners. The result is not primarily measured by mastering certain areas of expertise or a set of skills but a far more integrated kind of formation. Most strategically, such a pervasively integrated approach for how leaders are formed for the sake of God's mission in the world can overcome the two usual pitfalls: leaders who become overly assimilated to the culture of a congregation and community and thus lose any prophetic challenge *or* who feel impelled to impose prophetic challenges that are disconnected from what people are actually experiencing and interpreting in their life and world.

Distinctions between formation for clergy (or other rostered leaders) and lay formation for ministry become increasingly blurred. Seminary formation is no longer so separable from the formation of faith-practices of the rest of the people of God. There are more permeable boundaries between seminaries and the rest of the church and society, with a critical faith formation that increasingly is able to resist the pervasive domination of neoliberal ways of thinking, not only in society but also in churches. Fearful churches and seminaries are held captive to their own economic survival as institutions. Yet the credibility of the church will be viewed even more suspiciously than it is already if the unquestioned powers of domination with their assumptions and practices continue to hold sway over the church.

Admittedly, it may feel difficult to proclaim and live out this subversive message with those who pay your salary. Those who are freer from this dependency, such as those who are retired or who have other sources of income may feel and often are freer to do so, especially in non-stipendiary ways. However this wisdom and experience often doesn't count if it cannot be measured in financial terms, and typically are overlooked or sidelined. Those who are retired tend to be dismissed as "have beens," or no longer "active," rather than realizing they may be even more impelled by the Spirit, to take risks and work collaboratively rather than in threatening competition with others.

Some do not fit the mold or don't seem to fit in to established patterns and practices of church because they are from different races/ethnicities and class realities than those who have shaped and dominated the institutional church. Yet, their leadership may be especially needed if church is to become more subversive of unjust realities, and more genuinely multicultural rather than mono-cultural. What is crucial is the unleashing of imaginative creativity and locally-based collaboration for new points of entry and ways of being church.

This is not necessarily furthered through more funding or staffing beyond the congregation (church-wide, synodical, consultants). This may actually hamper rather than help, especially if it is suspected that "a plan" is being imposed on local ministry realities, and viewed as yet another instance of "top down" control or domination. Instead, more attention must be given to collaborative envisoning and pursuing ministry together—across established congregational lines—by those who are doing transformative ministry and who know it best (both clergy and lay). This is how faithfulness to the subversive boundary-crossing gospel happens, as an organic event, rather than through all the institutional trappings and expenses. People cannot be told from the outside, much less from above. What it means to be church today unfolds from the bottom/up, from inside/out into a much wider sense of catholicity.

As we have suggested here, intentionally pursuing practices of seeing–remembering–connecting with those among whom we minister can enable this more subversive message to be unfolded from within what they actually are experiencing and seeing, and from there to name the realities of what or who is dominating them. New insights into the liberating gospel can then be communicated in relation to these realities, as well as the connecting that is crucial for working with others to transform unjust realities.

The deeper connecting here also implies an end of "silo-ed" congregations, autonomous from others. These sites still often are sustained by perpetuating the illusion of a time when the church was big and prospering, but which can function as bulwarks against what lies outside. In contrast, Jesus was continually reversing who was outside and who was inside. It is not that these silos can be razed from above (e.g., by a church authority), but through pastoral/prophetic processes of being nurtured into a new reality—biblically based, theologically informed— of discipleship, in community, for the sake of the wider society, city, region, world. The catholicity of the church insists that a locale and its context are important but as interpenetrated with other realities and contexts. Without such a shift, congregations often remain root-bound and static, rather than dynamically enlivened by the Spirit who continually is putting us in relationship with others.

A wedge that must be challenged is that between more "traditional" congregations and more "emerging" ministries. Nor is the dichotomy between "spiritual" and "religious" helpful. The life of faith necessarily is communal, and need not be equated with institutional rigidities. *All* are emerging faith communities, in need of continual re-formation, rather than juxtaposed against each other. Again, this is not imposed from above by church authorities or designated experts. This is an awareness that grows slowly among those who are both inside and outside the organized church, together discerning what it means to be the church. Seeing–remembering–connecting can help unfold this—refocusing what faith communities are about, with a new awareness that comes from risky crossing of boundaries. This witnesses to what Jesus Christ is about—a "with-ness" rather than over and against others. The significant difference is not who is in or outside the institutional church (i.e., who is a "member"), but who participates in multifaceted transformative ventures that are impelled from out of the heart of the Good News, for the sake of the world, not just the church. The Spirit is making us misfits who are subversive of how things are—not over and against but in community with one another.

Leadership consequently looks much different. It is located not at the top of a hierarchical pyramid or organizational chart, but somewhere in the middle of what might be a rather messy circle in which lots of interconnections are continually being made among those who are part of the circle. It cannot really be charted because the connections that are being made across various relational transactions are changing continually, and are at the heart of what makes this deeply relational organization function. The leader(s) might be assumed to be the one making things move, but the Spirit-impelled energy and sense of purpose propelling it transcend who the leader is. She is often encouraging, suggesting directions, even herding from the midst of, rather than separate from or above the rest. She is steward of the connecting, relational power that is of the essence of the Triune God, not for the sake of profit, recognition or getting ahead of others, but through a connecting that empowers others, calling forth their gifts and vocation. It is a model that many feminist theologians have referred to as a round table rather than a hierarchical ladder of top down control.

Such leaders draw out and nurture those in the community who are likely to be the "seers, rememberers, and connectors," regardless of their status or official roles in the community. Seers are those who can see through the usual presumptions and illusions so as to name what is really going on. Rememberers are those who are able to make the past present, and remind us of those absent from "the table," for the sake of an unfolding future. Connectors are those who continually seek out and develop new working relationships, making connections with other people, organizations and movements, so as to work together for the common good. Bringing together those with gifts such as these, focused for the sake of God's mission in the world, through the synergistic dynamic of God's Spirit, can enliven the church far more than some of the usual practices that seek to sustain it as an institution.

In sum

If churches are to move from survival to engagement, some deeply embedded assumptions and practices need to change:

- instead of aspiring to be self-sufficient churches, our inter-relatedness;
- instead of being hostage to measures of "success," attitudes of humility shaped by a theology of the cross;
- instead of *our* strength or know-how, our vulnerability, open to listen and learn from others;
- instead of speaking and showing others, open to being transformed by those different from ourselves;
- instead of an insular sense of who we are as a church, open to how the Spirit of God continually is renewing, transforming the church through new faces and realities.

When fear of the future dominates the church, creative imagination shrinks. Ecclesial imagination requires putting ourselves in uncomfortable places, liminal spaces, at the intersections of many worlds. "It requires the retrieval of muted dangerous memories and the giving of [ourselves] fully to the demands of the future through active involvement in transforming actions in the present. . . . Imagination has no roots without memory, and without roots it does have wings to fly."[16]

Collaborative practices with others are "con-spiracy," which literally means "to breathe together." To "con-spire" is to share breath—life-affirming and liberating ways of thinking, dwelling, and acting. Such conspiracy or breathing together is necessary if we are to endure in the long struggle of resistance and transformation. Without the breath of our companions, we easily fall into fatigue and cynicism." Let our conspiracy of social imagination and transformation be a midwife for its birthing!"[17]

16. Fernandez, "Church as a Household," 186–87.
17. Ibid., 188.

Bibliography

Albrecht, Gloria. *The Character of Our Communities.* Nashville: Abingdon, 1995.

Altmann, Walter. "Justification in the Context of Exclusion—Latin America," In Wolfgang Greive, ed. 117–24. *Justification in the World's Context.* LWF Documentation Series 45. Geneva: Lutheran World Federation, 2000.

Bendroth, Margaret. *The Spiritual Practice of Remembering.* Grand Rapids: Eerdmans, 2013.

Bergmann, Sigurd. "Invoking the Spirit amid Dangerous Environmental Change." In *God, Creation and Climate Change,* edited by Karen L Bloomquist, 159–74. . LWF Studies. Geneva: Lutheran World Federation, 2009.

Best, Thomas, and Martin Robra. *Costly Obedience: Ecclesiology and Ethics.* Geneva: World Council of Churches, 1997.

Bitrus, Ibrahim S. "The Significance of the New Trinitarian Hermeneutics of God for Recasting the African Tradition of Community in Nigeria." PhD diss., Luther Seminary (St. Paul), 2015.

Bieler, Andrea, and Luise Schottroff. *The Eucharist: Bodies, Bread and Resurrection.* Minneapolis: Fortress, 2007.

Bloomquist, Karen L., ed. *Being the Church in the Midst of Empire: Trinitarian Reflections.* Theology in the Life of the Church 1. Minneapolis: Lutheran University Press and Geneva: Lutheran World Federation, 2007.

———. *The Dream Betrayed: Religious Challenge of the Working Class.* Minneapolis: Fortress, 1990.

———. "*Ekklesia* in the Midst of Moral Outrage Today." In *Dialog: A Journal of Theology* 51.1 (2012) 62–70.

———, ed. *God, Creation and Climate Change.* Minneapolis: Lutheran University Press, and Geneva: Lutheran World Federation, 2009.

———. "Lutheran Theology in the Future?" In *Transformative Theological Perspectives,* Karen L Bloomquist, 193–204. Theology in the Life of the Church 6. Minneapolis: Lutheran University Press and Geneva: Lutheran World Federation, 2009.

———. "Toward the Redemption of White American Working-Class Experience: A Liberation Theology." Ph.D. diss., Union Theological Seminary (NYC), 1985.

————, ed. *Transformative Theological Perspectives*. Theology in the Life of the Church 6. Minneapolis: Lutheran University Press and Geneva: Lutheran World Federation, 2009.

————. "Transforming Domination Then and Now." In *Lutheran Identity and Political Theology*, Carl-Henric Grenholm and Goran Gunner, 208–21. Eugene OR: Pickwick Publications, 2014.

Bloomquist, Karen L., and Ulrich Duchrow, eds. *Church–Liberated for Resistance and Transformation*. De Reformation radikalisieren 5. Münster: Lit, 2015.

Bloomquist, Karen L., and John R. Stumme, eds. *The Promise of Lutheran Ethics*. Minneapolis: Fortress, 1998.

Brooks, David. "The Structure of Gratitude." *New York Times*. July 28, 2015. http://www.nytimes.com/2015/07/28/opinion/david-brooks-the-structure-of-gratitude.html.

Brueggemann, Walter. *Journey to the Common Good*. Louisville: Westminster John Knox, 2010.

————. *Out of Babylon*. Nashville: Abingdon, 2010.

————. *Truth-Telling as Subversive Obedience*. Edited by K. C. Hanson. Eugene, OR: Cascade Books, 2011.

————. *The Word Militant: Preaching a Decentering Word*. Minneapolis: Fortress, 2010.

Carter, Warren. *John and Empire*. London: T & T Clark, 2008.

Carter, Jimmy. Interview on Thom Hartmann program, July 28 2015. http://www.thomhartmann.com/bigpicture/president-jimmy-carter-united-states-oligarchy.

Cavanaugh, William. *Torture and Eucharist*. London: Blackwell, 1998.

Centre for Living Christianity. http://livingchristianityscotland.word press. com/.

Chung, Paul S. *Church and Ethical Responsibility in the Midst of World Economy*. Eugene, OR: Cascade Books, 2013.

Chung, Paul S., Ulrich Duchrow, and Craig L. Nessan. *Liberating Lutheran Theology: Freedom for Justice and Solidarity with Others in a Global Context*. Studies in Lutheran History and Theology. Minneapolis: Fortress 2011.

deChristopher, Tim. "The Value of Protest," July 14, 2015. http://www.timdechristopher.org/the_value_of_protest.

deYoung, Curtiss Paul, Michael O. Emerson, and George Yancy. *United by Faith: The Multicultural Congregation as an Answer to the Problem of Race*. New York: Oxford, 2003.

Driver, Tom F. *Patterns of Grace: Human Experience as Word of God*. San Francisco: Harper & Row, 1977.

Ellison, Keith, and Van Jones. "Pollution Isn't Colorblind." *Guardian UK*: July 23 2015. http://www.theguardian.com/commentisfree/2015/jul/23/black-lives-matter-air-pollution.

Evangelical Lutheran Church in America. "Abortion." http://www.elca.org/Faith/Faith-and-Society/Social-Statements/Abortion.

Evangelical Lutheran Church in America. "Sufficient, Sustainable Livelihoood for All." www.elca.org/Faith/Faith-and-Society/Social-Statements/Economic-Life.

Fernandez, Eleazar S. "The Church as a Household of Life Abundant." In Kathleen Ray Darby, ed. 172–88. *Theology That Matters: Ecology, Economy, and God.* Minneapolis: Fortress, 2006.

Francis, Pope. *Laudato Si.* http://w2.vatican.va/content/francesco/en/encyclicals/documents/papa-francesco_20150524_enciclica-laudato-si.html.

Fredrickson, David E. "Free Speech in Pauline Political Theology." In *Word and World* 12 (1992) 345–51.

———. "Pauline Ethics." In *The Promise of Lutheran Ethics*, edited by Karen L. Bloomquist and John R. Stumme, 115–29. Minneapolis: Fortress, 1998.

Giroux, Henry. "The Violence of Organized Forgetting." July 22, 2013. http://www.truth-out.org/op-ed/item/17647-the-violence-of-organized-forgetting.

———. "Living in the Age of Imposed Amnesia." Nov. 16, 2010. http://www.truth-out.org.

Greive, Wolfgang, ed. *Justification in the World's Context.* LWF Documentation Series 45. Geneva: Lutheran World Federation, 2000.

Grenholm, Carl-Henric, and Goran Gunner, eds. *Lutheran Identity and Political Theology.* Church of Sweden Research Series 9. Eugene, OR: Pickwick Publications, 2014.

Grosshans, Hans-Peter, ed. *One Holy Catholic Apostolic Church: Some Lutheran and Ecumenical Perspectives.* LWF Studies 1/2009. Geneva: Lutheran World Federation, 2009.

Hallowell, Edward. "Connectedness." In *Finding the Heart of the Child.* Braintree, MA: Association of Independent Schools in New England, Inc., 1993.

Hansen, Guillermo. "Resistance, Adaptation or Challenge: The Versatility of the Lutheran Code." In *Transformative Theological Perspectives*, edited by Karen L Bloomquist, 23–38. Theology in the Life of the Church 6. Minneapolis: Lutheran University Press and Geneva: Lutheran World Federation, 2009.

Hedges, Chris. *Empire of Illusion: The End of Literacy and the Rise of Spectacle.* New York: Nation, 2009.

Hendrix, Scott. *Luther and the Papacy.* Minneapolis: Fortress, 1981.

Horsley, Richard, and Neil Asher Silberman. *The Message and the Kingdom: How Jesus and Paul Ignited a Revolution and Transformed the Ancient World.* 1997. Reprinted, Minneapolis: Fortress, 2002.

Jenning, Willie J. *The Christian Imagination: Theology and the Origins of Race.* New Haven: Yale University Press, 2010.

Kahl, Brigitte. *Galatians Re-Imagined: Reading with the Eyes of the Vanquished.* Minneapolis: Fortress, 2010.

Killen, Patricia O'Connell. "Memory, Novelty and Possibility in This Place." In *Cascadia: The Elusive Utopia*, edited by Douglas Todd, 65–85. Vancouver BC: Ronsdale, 2008.

Klein, Naomi. "People and Planet First." http://readersupportednews.org/opinion2/277-75/31064-people-and-planet-first.

————. "A Radical Vatican." *The New Yorker*, 11 July 2015. http://www.newyorker.com/news/news-desk/a-visit-to-the-vatican

Kolb, Robert, and Timothy J. Wengert, eds. *The Book of Concord: The Confessions of the Evangelical Lutheran Church*. Translations by Charles Arand. Minneapolis: Fortress, 2000.

Kotsko, Adam. *The Politics of Redemption: The Social Logic of Salvation*. London: T & T Clarke, 2010.

Kruse, Kevin M. "A Christian Nation? Since When?" *The New York Times*, March 15, 2015. http://www.nytimes.com/2015/03/15/opinion/sunday/a-christian-nation-since-when.html.

Laarman, Peter. "Humiliation and 'Success' in the Great Recession." *Religious Dispatches*, September 6, 2011. http://religiondispatches.org/?s=Peter+La arman%2C+September+6%2C+2011.

LaCugna, Catherine. *God for Us: The Trinity and Christian Life*. San Francisco: Harper, 1991.

Lewis, Alan E. *Between Cross and Resurrection: A Theology of Holy Saturday*. Grand Rapids: Eerdmans, 2001.

Lindberg, Carter. "Luther on Poverty." In *Harvesting Martin Luther's Reflections on Theology, Ethics, and the Church*, edited by Timothy J. Wengert, 134–51. Grand Rapids: Eerdmans, 2004.

Luther, Martin. *Luther's Works*. American edition. Vols. 1–30, Jaroslav Pelikan, general ed. St. Louis: Concordia, 1955–67. Vol. 31–35, Helmut T. Lehmann, general ed. Philadelphia: Fortress, 1955–86.

Lutheran World Federation. "Daily Bread Instead of Greed." Public statement of the 2010 Assembly. http.://, www.lwf-assembly.org/assembly-documents.

————. "Message of the Tenth Assembly (2003)." http://lwf-assembly2003.org/lwf-assembly/htdocs/PDFs/LWF_Assembly_Message-EN.pdf

Lyon, David. *The Silicon Society*. London Lectures in Contemporary Society. Grand Rapids: Eerdmans, 1986.

Magoda, James. "Uganda: Our Leaders Suffer from Social Amnesia." *Observer* (Kampala), 23 Sept. 2009.

Mahn, Jason A. "What are Churches *For?* Toward an Ecclesiology of the Cross after Christendom." *Dialog* 51.1 (2012) 14–23.

McFague, Sallie. *A New Climate for Theology: God, the World, and Climate Warming*. Minneapolis: Fortress, 2008.

McLaren, Brian D. *Why Did Jesus, Moses, the Buddha, and Mohammed Cross the Road? Christian Identity in a Multifaith World*. New York: Jericho, 2012.

Metz, Johann Baptist. *Faith in History and Society*. New York: Seabury, 1980.

Miguez, Nestor, Joerg Rieger, and Jung Mo Sung. *Beyond the Spirit of Empire*. Louisville: Westminster John Knox, 2009.

Moe-Lobeda, Cynthia D. "*Communio* and a Spirituality of Resistance." In *Communion, Responsibility, Accountability*, edited by Karen L. Bloomquist, ed. 145–56. LWF Documentation 50. Geneva: Lutheran World Federation, 2004.

———. *Healing a Broken World: Globalization and God*. Minneapolis: Fortress, 2002.

———. *Resisting Structural Evil: Love as Ecological-Economic Vocation*. Minneapolis: Fortress, 2013.

Moltmann, Jürgen. *The Church in the Power of the Spirit: A Contribution to Messianic Ecclesiology*. Translated by Margaret Kohl. 1977. Reprinted, Minneapolis: Fortress, 1993.

———. *The Trinity and the Kingdom: The Doctrine of God*. Translated by Margaret Kohl. 1981. Reprinted, Minneapolis: Fortress, 1993.

Nessan, Craig L. *Shalom Church: The Body of Christ as Ministering Community*. Minneapolis: Fortress, 2010.

Niebuhr, H. Richard. *Christ and Culture*. New York: Harper, 1951.

O'Day, Gail R. "John." In *The New Interpreter's Bible*, edited by Leander E. Keck, 9:491–864. Nashville: Abingdon 1996.

Patton, John. *Pastoral Care in Context*. Louisville: Westminster John Knox, 1993.

Pickard, Stephen. *Seeking the Church: An Introduction to Ecclesiology*. London: SCM, 2012.

Powell, Lewis. "Confidential Memorandum (August 23, 1971): Attack on the Free Enterprise System." In *Invisible Hands: The Making of the Conservative Movement from the New Deal to Reagan*, by Kim Phelps-Fein. New York: Norton, 2009.

"Radicalizing Reformation—Provoked by the Bible and Today's Crises." http://www.radicalizing-reformation.com/index.php/en/.

Ray, Darby, Kathleen Ray, ed. *Theology That Matters: Ecology, Economy, and God*. Minneapolis: Fortress, 2006.

Rieger, Joerg. *No Rising Tide: Theology, Economics, and the Future*. Minneapolis: Fortress, 2009.

Russell, Letty M. *Church in the Round: Feminist Interpretation of the Church*. Louisville: Westminster John Knox, 1993.

Schmiechen, Peter. *Christ the Reconciler: A Theology for Opposites, Differences, and Enemies*. Grand Rapids: Eerdmans, 1996.

Scott, Margaret. *The Eucharist and Social Justice*. New York: Paulist, 2009.

Schultze, Quentin. *Habits of the High-Tech Heart*. Grand Rapids: Eerdmans, 2002.

Schwartz, Regina M. *Sacramental Poetics at the Dawn of Secularism: When God Left the World*. Palo Alto: Stanford University Press, 2008.

Soelle, Dorothee. *Political Theology*. Translated by John Shelley. Philadelphia: Fortress, 1974.

———. *The Silent Cry: Mysticism and Resistance*. Minneapolis: Fortress, 2001.

————. *Thinking about God: An Introduction to Theology.* Translated by John Bowden. Philadelphia: Trinity, 1990.

Solberg, Mary. *Compelling Knowledge: A Feminist Proposal for an Epistemology of the Cross.* Albany: State University of New York, 1997.

Tiede, David L. "Justifying Faith and the Net Worth of Productivity—USA." In *Justification in the World's Context,* edited by Wolfgang Greive, 103–15. LWF Documentation 45. Geneva: Lutheran World Federation, 2000.

Todd, Douglas, ed. *Cascadia: The Elusive Utopia.* Vancouver BC: Ronsdale, 2008.

Wasik, Bill. "Welcome to the Age of Digital Imperialism." June 7, 2015. http://www.nytimes.com/2015/06/07/magazine/welcome-to-the-age-of-digital-imperialism.html.

Wengert, Timothy J., ed. *Harvesting Martin Luther's Reflections on Theology, Ethics, and the Church.* Grand Rapids: Eerdmans, 2004.

Westhelle, Vitor. "The Priesthood of All Believers." In *Church–Liberated for Resistance and Transformation,* edited by Karen L. Bloomquist and Ulrich Duchrow, 179–190. Die Reformation radikalisieren 5. Münster: Lit, 2015.

————. *The Scandalous God: The Use and Abuse of the Cross.* Minne-apolis: Fortress, 2006.

Wilkinson, Richard, and Kate Pickett. "How Inequality Hollows Out the Soul." In "The Great Divide," *New York Times,* February 2, 2014. http://opinionator.blogs.nytimes.com/2014/02/02/how-inequality-hollows-out-the-soul/.

World Alliance of Reformed Churches. "Accra Confession (2004)." http://wcra.ch/accra/the-accra-confession.